LEADERSHIP EXCELLENCE IN PERSONAL DEVELOPMENT

DR GAJANAN SHIRKE

Contents

Acknowledgements

I would like to express a special debt of gratitude to my wife Rajeshree and my two daughters Rupeshi & Kavya, my teammates and superior leaders who encourages me to write.

About Book

Leadership Excellence in Personal Development is a book which is set out to teach you the principles of personal leadership. We live in an age where everything seems to have advanced, everything. Tasks that used to take almost eternity are now accomplished almost immediately. Human, through the aid of technology, has redefined life. Things our ancestors tagged impossible we now take for granted. Indeed life has advanced beyond imagination. This book is very simple to understand by all. But if you will just take your time to live them out you'll be amazed at the changes you will experience in your life. Dr Gajanan Shirke demonstrates the process of personal transformation, book explains the value of psychology and spirituality for leadership roles, and presents a pioneering and refreshed vision of leadership that meets present global demands for social cohesion and sustainability. This edition contains updates throughout and presents personal narratives that illustrate the virtues of leadership practice in our current socio-political context. This book addresses questions on how leadership is defined, exercised and communicated in contemporary society.

About The Author

Dr Gajanan Shirke, a hotel consultant, has years of extensive experience in the hospitality industry. His thirst for learning and aspiration to become a multi-faceted expert in the hotel industry helped him rise from employment to becoming an independent professional in the hospitality sector. Since his last assignment as General Manager at Kamat Hotels, he has become a renowned hotel consultant with a proven track record of developing, training and growing some of the best-known hotels, restaurants and fast-food joints in the Indian market. He was appointed as an expert consultant for The Eighth meeting of the Board of Studies for Hotel Management & Catering Technology. He is a visiting faculty at various Hotel Management Colleges and has trained over a thousand hospitality professionals. He has completed numerous pre and post opening hotel consultancies in India and overseas.

In order to spread his extensive knowledge to aspiring hotel professionals, Gajanan has penned a large number of books spanning different segments of the hospitality industry. Starting from his first book 'Bar Management and Operations' published in 2010, he has written 48 books including Hospitality Management, Food and Beverage Management, Hotel Engineering Management, Front Office Management, Hotel Housekeeping Management, The Cookery Trilogy: Advance Cookery Theory, The Cookery Trilogy: Foundation of Cookery, The Cookery Trilogy: The Basic Cookery Book, Hotel Sales and Marketing, Hospitality Industry Accounting & Fundamentals, Customer Interaction Excellence in Hospitality, History of Indian Cuisine – Volume 1, History of Indian Cuisine – Volume 2, Hotel Owner's Manual, Hotel Security & Prevention, Training Manager's Manual, Exceptional Service In Hospitality Six Sigma Way, etc.

Index

CHAPTER ONE

Attention Management

THERE ARE 86400 Seconds in a day, and regardless of what fills those minutes, we all have a limited amount of time to get things done. Managers and leaders often use a plethora of buzzwords in an attempt to effectively manage our time, prioritize tasks, and disconnect when our window closes. But is that enough? The theory of time management came about during the Industrial Revolution and the rise of employment in factories when people had to learn to "live by the clock rather than live by the sun." In 1911, Fredrick Winslow published "The Principles of Scientific Management" for managers to analyze the best way for workers to complete their jobs and separate actions to eliminate unnecessary motions.

Today, we block our schedules to complete tasks based on what we believe to be an adequate window. We believe when the time allocated elapses, we should be done. Often, that is not the case. In most cases, we do not get anywhere close to completing the task, which leaves us scrambling to find more time in our calendars to finish the task we planned to finish. Are we just less effective today than our predecessors? Time management has had its place since the Industrial Revolution and was an effective theory until the emergence of the Digital Revolution, also known as the Third Industrial Revolution. Present-day concepts of time management are not only ineffective but have created more problems than solutions. This theory fails in our personal and professional lives due to the digital age we live in. We are inundated with notifications and information. Our phones, tablets, watches, and computers alert us to everything going on around us. The irony is that we use these devices to "enhance" our lives. However, these are the culprits to reducing our focus.

Scientific studies show that the term "multitasking" is a fallacy that we allow ourselves to believe. When we multitask, we feel that we are completing tasks faster, therefore, getting more done. According to research, our brain can focus only on a single task. The next time you think you're multitasking, you are actually just switching back and forth between multiple singular tasks repeatedly. The truth is multitasking results in wasted time due to context switching, and our work becomes prone to increased errors. When multitasking, our brain hits a bottleneck that does not allow information processing for two simultaneous tasks, leaving only the most essential information. Attention economics is an approach to managing information that treats human attention as a scarce commodity and applies economic theory to solve various information management problems. Attention is a resource – a person has only so much of it. Attention is focused mental engagement on a particular item of information. Items come into our awareness, we attend to a particular item, and then we decide whether to act. As alerts, phone calls, texts, and other previously unavailable distractions become a part of our everyday lives; attention becomes a limiting factor as we try to consume information. Our brain filters information by putting the most vital information first while leaving other details out. Now, it is said that the genuine cost of multitasking can cause you to lose 40% of productivity. The Institute of Psychiatry found that multitasking shows a temporary ten-point drop in IQ, more than our mental effectiveness while under the influence of marijuana. Additionally, a study completed by the University of California at Irvine monitored interruptions among office workers. This study found that workers were interrupted, on average, every 11 minutes. The study also found that it took 23 minutes to return to their original task.

This "task switching" involves several parts of your brain, including the prefrontal cortex that is involved in switching and focusing attention, the posterior parietal lobe, which activates rules for each task you switch to, the anterior cingulate gyrus monitors for errors, and the pre-motor cortex prepares for you to move. Given that attention is a cognitive process involving a selective concentration of resources and information, attention can be considered a limited resource. After examining what science says about our ability to multitask, we know that we cannot, but we continue to apply multitasking to every part of our lives. The question now becomes why. Why do we think we can multitask even when all the information tells us we cannot? A dopamine-driven feedback loop is a self-perpetuating circuit fueled by how the neurotransmitter works with the brain's reward system. Feedback loops, in general, are circuits that return output as input to a given system to drive future operations and, in this case, behaviors.

Dopamine is associated with "seeking" behavior. Once we feel that we have a perceived accomplishment through multitasking, dopamine is released, and we reengage in the behavior to release more dopamine.

Social media is an example of a dopamine feedback look. We search for entertainment or information as we scroll through our social media newsfeeds in anticipation of pleasure when something we seek pops up. The number of interesting posts in the newsfeed does not matter because intermittent reinforcement of finding relevant posts reinforces the behavior and subsequent dopamine release. Because our body does not have a mechanism for satiety built-in, the dopamine feedback loop allows the behavior to continue for much longer than we intend and much longer than the perceived psychological rewards. Now that we know the issues with time management and why those issues exist, is there any hope in how to manage our time more constructively? The answer is yes! By moving away from the concept of time management to a new philosophy: attention management. Attention management adapts how we allocate our time and uses other methods to reduce our need to divide our attention during our tasks.

First things first, when you are working on something that requires a high focus, turn off your notifications. Seriously ... how often do you get a notification that requires your immediate attention? Let people know to call you if there is an emergency but set boundaries on the definition of an emergency. This will be extremely tough at first. Remember the dopamine loop? It will nag at you, but letting go of your notifications on your phone, watch, and computer is freedom you may not realize exists. Second, you must set boundaries. You cannot achieve focus without boundaries. Without focus, you are multitasking. Set up designated times for your team to meet with you. Instead of having others figure out your calendar, set a daily or weekly time designated for this purpose. This allows you to completely focus on the team's needs instead of being partially available because you are not focused. How often does someone come into your office, and you have a complete conversation while trying to send an important email? When the conversation is over, what was in the email? What was the outcome of the conversation? You probably have no idea.

Set focus times for specific tasks. Find out where your values are and prioritize your day on those values. For example, if you know you need to keep your email checked, set focus time twice a day where you only go through your email. Turn off the notifications, close the door, eliminate distractions, and get it done. Also, create procedures within the organization, when emailing, to carbon copy (cc) team members that may need to know the information, but it is not a priority and does not need action or response. Set rules in your email to send the cc'd email to its own inbox that you check every few days.

In summary, multitasking is not an effective way to manage our daily workloads. Our brains have a limited capacity to process information, and multitasking further reduces our productivity and quality of work. With this knowledge, our best approach to managing our tasks is to create opportunities to focus on the tasks we need to complete or value the most. Finding ways to create focus time is most effective when we create boundaries, develop procedures on communicating internally (i.e., when to call, email, and carbon copy), and commit to the time to focus on a single task. As organizations are having difficulty finding talent in today's labor market, many leaders are looking for a way to manage their existing teams' capacity. While time management was effective in the past, our digital world has changed how we should manage our time and attention.

Four Areas of Attention:

Intentional: When working intentionally, people plan strategically and prioritize their activities.

Responsive: In this area people are responding to the world around them. They spend more time putting out fires than working intentionally.

Interrupted: People spend too much time answering messages and handling situations that interrupt their work.

Unproductive: This occurs when people waste time at work. Unless you are taking a scheduled break, checking Facebook and chatting is unproductive.

Stop Thinking and Pay Attention!

The advice "stop thinking" may seem counterintuitive to attention management. Many people, however, are over thinking everything and focused on the wrong ideas. When we constantly think we do not pay attention to what is really going on around us. Our feelings control how and what we think. If we think that something is boring, bad, or a waste of time, we tend to give it less attention. For example, people are less likely to pay attention during a meeting if they believe it will not be productive. The ability to pay attention allows people to better connect with the world around them, better process their emotions, and organize the way they process cognitively

Manage your attention by taking steps like these:

- Does your team frequently interrupt you to get your input? Make sure they understand which decisions they are empowered to make on their own. You could also ask them to hold non-urgent questions until their weekly one-on-one with you. It's more important to your leadership role that you have thoughtful time, and that they know you trust their judgement to make their own decisions.
- Overwhelmed by email? Give yourself more "unplugged" time, and "retrain" the people around you that you don't answer emails immediately. (And if you're lucky, this will have a ripple effect in the office, helping to make everyone more thoughtfully responsive rather than blindly reactive.)
- Is your own restless mind your number one distraction? If so, you're not alone. With all the interruptions in our lives, our minds get addicted to them. So, when we do get a rare quiet moment, we sabotage ourselves with impulses like "I should Google those movie times for this weekend" or "I wonder what's happening on social media." The good news is you can rebuild your focus muscle. As a first step, turn off all notifications, set a timer for 10 minutes and focus on a single task.

All of these strategies help put you back in charge of your own attention. And you can start using them right away. As you do, you'll free up more time for your most important work and for becoming the most effective leader you can be.

Be accountability buddies for each other: People don't give the daily stand-up enough credit. Sure, it's a quick way to get status updates, but it's also a gentle accountability mechanism. As each person shares their progress since last time and plan for today, the manager or project lead has an opportunity to make sure everyone is focused on the most important work and help course-correct if needed. For agile teams, your sprint planning session can serve the same purpose, and in a more proactive way, to boot.

Stay connected to the "why": When you're trying to push a big rock up a hill, at some point (like when your legs cramp up) you're going to wonder if the payoff is really worth all this effort. When that moment comes, a sharp sense of purpose will help you resist the temptation to prop the rock in place and go lie down and watch a cat video. Whatever your team's "big rock" is, everyone should have a shared understanding of why you're tackling it. If you haven't already, spend a few minutes in your next team or project meeting discussing that. Then, as you go along, put that "why" statement at the top of every document, chart, Slack channel, and slide deck related to the project for reinforcement.

CHAPTER TWO

Being Likeable Boss

One of the biggest fallacies you'll hear about good managers is that they usually aren't very likable; that the most effective bosses are usually tyrants who put the success of the business ahead of being nice to their employees. That's absolutely untrue, especially in today's workplace. In the modern business world, so much relies on a boss' ability to not only motivate workers but also keep them happy – especially the best ones. With all the job-hopping that goes on these days, bosses you aren't able to retain their best employees simply can't be viewed as being successful at managing their staff, regardless of whether the business is making money or not. Employees, especially great ones, are a huge commodity these days, and according to many surveys, like this one, employees tend to run from companies that have unlikable bosses. If your employee do not feel that you are a supportive and good leader, they are not going to work hard for you and they are definitely not going to stay loyal to your company for long. Studies have shown that great bosses lead to better employee engagement. As the business world evolves, so does the definition of a "great boss." Bosses and high-level managers have very diversified roles these days and responsibilities that are constantly changing and morphing into something new.

A great boss needs to create an atmosphere in which employees are empowered and motivated to perform well. Great managers are able to create a healthy atmosphere where teamwork is naturally promoted and healthy competition is easily achieved. Good managers need to know their staff well and employees need to trust their leadership. The team needs to be united under one flag, collaboration needs to be organic and there needs to be a high level of good communication and transparency present across all levels of the company. Great bosses are proactive when addressing team needs, problems or shortcomings. They are able to achieve a positive workplace atmosphere in which employees are engaged and motivated to work hard. And in the end, all of these goals can be much more easily achieved if your employees like you. Contrary to popular belief, a likable boss is not a pushover. Your team can like you and respect you at the same time. It's all depends on whether or not you are gaining their respect and admiration the right way.

For leaders to lead effectively, they need to do a self-introspection and fix their own behaviours first. In order to build a great workplace, you must first build yourself by gaining a deep understanding of your strengths and weaknesses as a leader, and you must completely commit to developing yourself into the best leader and person you can be. At the same time, you must hire outstanding people who are as committed as you are to build a great workplace.

Prompt and timely feedback is more important than anything else. Try to provide one-on-one coaching and development chats regularly. Sharing periodic feedback will help employee development and help them learn from mistakes whilst building their confidence and vice-versa. Always be transparent, honest, and constructive. A great boss will be open-minded, so allow your employees to provide feedback by creating a safe and open space to do so. By practicing open communication, you will help build trust with your employees and improve overall work morale.

A great boss will always remember that employees in any team size are still unique individuals, a complete entity in their own selves, with their typical strengths and weaknesses. People under pressure usually forget this. So, you must remember to personalize your interactions with each employee, a unique bond and understanding with each one of them. Take into consideration their varying interests, abilities, goals and ways of learning to ensure you can have a meaningful impact when conversing, training and teaching them.

Most of the time, bosses claim that they want their employees to contribute new ideas, take initiatives, and so on and so forth but in reality, they don't practice. If your employees start feeling that you don't care for their views and knock down their ideas, they may never come forward offering new ideas or suggestions for that matter. Instead of enforcing all of your ideas, try actively listening to your employees' fresh ideas and perspectives. You might be surprised by the solutions they come up with for daily problems the business faces.

When you are responsible for overseeing a large number of employees or projects, you might be tempted to follow a very prescriptive format. While there are benefits to having a set of processes, it's also to maintain enough flexibility to counteract the occasional surprise that is bound to arise from time to time. Similarly, avoid micromanaging your teams any more than you have to, as this can negatively impact morale and productivity. Give them their space and let them make mistakes and learn from those.

Giving Your Employees Independence: We've talked a lot already about empowering employees in order to motivate them to succeed. To that end, there's nothing more empowering than giving your employees a higher level of independence in their day-to-day responsibilities. Giving employees independence is not about letting them do what they want without having to listen to anyone in management, it's about guiding them to do the right things without having to explicitly order them to do so. Most of all, it's about trusting them to make the right decisions and doing the right things independently.

This is what most employees crave, especially Millennials. Younger workers want challenges and they want the ability to showcase their talents. That's why loosening the grip a bit is necessary step that all good bosses must take. Employees thrive in an atmosphere in which managers encourage them to work more independently and trust their instincts. According to this study, giving your employees more autonomy not only motivates them, it also keeps them happy. Of course, with additional independence you are increasing the chances of employees making mistakes. But that's completely fine. The trick is in handling these mistakes the right way. Beloved bosses know how to deal with employee mistakes the right way. The last thing you want to breed is an atmosphere in which your staff members are afraid to make mistakes because they are terrified of your potential reaction to the error. When employees are afraid to make mistakes, they usually end up doing a lot less at work. The best and most well-liked bosses encourage employees to experiment and fail, but also know how to react to these mistakes and coach their staff members to use them as learning experiences that will make them better workers in the long run.

Know everyone's Role: Employees love bosses who actually understand what everyone's role in the company entails. A good boss is able to relate to what you are working on and also empathize with and understand any of the problems you might be going through as a worker. If you don't understand the work that your employees are doing, it's going to be hard for you to relate to them and understand their needs. Of course, no one can be an expert on everything, but it doesn't hurt to at least know the basics.

For example, most restaurant employees say that the best bosses are the ones who have previous experience working as hourly employees in restaurants before graduating to managerial roles. They have an in-depth understanding of what it takes to run a successful restaurant from the inside and they are able to empathize with the struggles that their workers face on a day-to-day basis. When you know about the challenges they face and you are able to coach them along the way instead of just barking out orders and setting deadlines, you're able to achieve a sort of "comfort zone" in the workplace. This usually results in coming across to your staff as a more relatable and understanding boss.

Make Good Communication a Priority: Likable bosses understand that good communication is a need foundation for team success. They want to hear input from their employees, they value the opinions of their staff and they want to keep the lines of communication open in order to achieve an atmosphere of transparency and trust across the board.

Great communication is important for a lot of reasons. Bosses who are good communicators are more trusted by their team. Employees who are always on the same page as their bosses are inherently happier at work because of it and having good communication makes it easier to avoid or defuse conflicts in the workplace if they do arise. Employees don't like to work in a state of ambiguity. They thrive when the lines of communication are open between management and staff and feel empowered when they are encouraged to share their thoughts, questions and even criticisms with management. When bosses care enough to openly ask employees for feedback, it gives staff members the feeling that they are respected and truly needed in the workplace, which directly inspires and motivates them to achieve their potential.

Be Reliable: Employees love it when they know what they are getting with a boss. They value consistency because knowing what to expect from management can definitely decrease stress levels at work, compared to having a boss who is your best buddy one day and screaming at you the next. One study shows that employees who are treated inconsistently end up experiencing significantly more stress at work than both employees who are consistently treated fairly or even unfairly.

Employees like bosses who walk the walk. Good bosses are consistent, stick to their plans and are true to their words. Bosses who don't waver in their decision-making become role models and are more readily viewed as strong leaders. Consistency also earns the respect of your employees. If you want your staff to love you, be a man or woman of your word and earn their trust by being steadfast and honorable in every decision that you make. The less erratic you are, the more comfortable your employees will feel around you and the more they will trust you and enjoy working for you.

CHAPTER THREE

Critical Thinking

Critical thinking is the ability to think clearly and rationally; it includes the ability to engage in reflective and independent thinking. A leader with critical thinking skills can understand the logical connections between ideas, identify the relevance and importance of arguments, detect inconsistencies or mistakes in reasoning, and make proper decisions. I am sure you have met leaders that are clearly intelligent and good at coming up with the right answer, but make questionable decisions. I have met leaders over the years who have had great people skills, could inspire those around them and were good at implementing solutions. However, those same leaders were incapable of thinking through the implications of a potential scenario, could not properly evaluate options they were faced with, or detect a flaw in someone else's logic, and often made wrong decisions, displaying their lack of critical thinking skills.

To be a good critical thinker, you have to be able to not only gather information but assess the relevance of these options. How critical are they to the situation and which piece of information will have the most impact on the problem at hand. How probable is one consequence over another? Which assumptions can you rely upon and what are the ones you should question? All of these are important questions that help people refine their judgment and make thoughtful decisions. In today's fast-changing and highly competitive business environment, the risks of poor decisions are greater than ever. Leaders have to make decisions about their organization's strategic direction, competitive positioning and proper allocation of resources. In most cases, leaders cannot rely on what has worked in the past, as the business challenges they are facing are new and ever-changing. Therefore, they have to be able to adequately assess options, potential consequences, and promptly adjust to new information in order to ensure they consistently make the right decisions. When poor decisions are made an organization may compromise their reputation and miss critical opportunities. In a world of constant change you need powerful tools for building enduring business.Having had the experience of resolving an issue in the past, does not guarantee success in the future as too many parameters have changed. This is why our assessments, whether they serve a selection or development purpose, measure a leader's ability to conceptualize, synthesize, and evaluate information to reach the proper conclusion. By using a combination of tools – including cognitive tests, case studies, management simulations and behavioural interview questions – we are able to assess how someone processes information, selects the most relevant elements and makes the right decision consistently, and throughout different settings. And that is a key quality that can turn a struggling leader into an exceptional one.

By taking responsibility for your own leadership critical thinking processes, you are taking action to analyse and adapt your approach to decision-making and problem-solving. You put yourself - and your company - in a much stronger position to lead and succeed in the "new normal" business world. There is a growing recognition that the old, pre-crisis way of doing business is never coming back. In its place is the "new normal". While some classic leadership strategies and skills will continue to be effective, leaders in this brave new world will need to lead differently - and think differently.

Critical thinking enables leaders at every level to understand the impact of their decisions on the business as a whole and ensures both alignment with organisational goals and accountability for results. The "new normal" is a different kind of competitive landscape, buffeted by geopolitics and global instability, rapid technological change, unique financial pressures, a rising tide of data and information to filter through, and the proliferation of new corporate business models. The mind-set that made leaders successful in the past probably won't ensure success in the future. In fact, several recent studies and surveys have identified critical thinking as the number one requirement for successful leadership in the 21st century. Yet there is mounting evidence that many current and emerging leaders lack this quality. And it is this competency gap that is shaking up and reshaping leadership as we have come to know it.

Help your team members learn to be critical thinkers: If you're in a leadership role, teach your team members how to think more critically and objectively. Having a team of critical thinkers will make them more effective and efficient. Teaching others a skill will also make you stronger at that skill yourself. If your actions inspire others to dream more, learn more, do more and become more, you are a leader.

Critical thinking is critical: Critical thinking appears to be exactly what is needed from leaders who are navigating the volatility of the "new normal. Critical thinking is the use of those cognitive skills or strategies that increase the probability of a desirable outcome. It is used to describe thinking that is purposeful, reasoned, and goal-directed - the kind of thinking involved in solving problems, formulating inferences, calculating likelihoods, and making decisions ... it's the kind of thinking that makes desirable outcomes more likely.

Implementing critical thinking needs unidentified problems. Individuals who are able to think critically use the cognitive skills like recognizing valid and invalid generalizations used in scientific processes, analyzing and evaluating opinions, analyzing interdisciplinary regression, rational interpretation, determining and evaluating the assumptions. Also, it is expressed that mental maturity at critical thinking is an important factor that affects the success . Critical thinking is the most advanced form of thinking because, it means objective, unprejudiced and in-depth thinking. Through critical thinking we can distinguish the qualified from the unqualified and right from the wrong. Critical thinking is a way of thinking which reaches to the core of the problem, examines them from different angles and if necessary opposes them. Sense of freedom and the thrill of discovering something makes critical thinking pleasant. According to Glaser and Watson, critical thinking skills contain sub-scales of problem recognization, ability to choose the appropriate information for problem solving, ability to consider specific or unspecific conditions and selecting, formulating and hypothesizing the relevant information and justifying the validity of the results. Acquisition of these skills may be possible through a well planned student centered education and by using methods and approaches where students actively participate in learning activities. The general idea at critical thinking is judging the thing what was done or believed in a reflective way. In the center of critical thinking exist analysis of cognitive skills, interpretation, inference, explanation, evaluation and verification and monitoring of one's self.

Critical thinking skills

Critical thinking is a soft skill that comprises multiple interpersonal and analytical abilities and attributes. Here are some essential critical thinking skills that can support workforce success.

- **Observation:** Employees with critical thinking can easily sense and identify an existing problem – and even predict potential issues – based on their experience and sharp perception. They're willing to embrace multiple points of view and look at the big picture.
- **Analytical thinking:** Analytical thinkers collect data from multiple sources, reject bias, and ask thoughtful questions. When approaching a problem, they gather and double-check facts, assess independent research, and sift through information to determine what's accurate and what can help resolve the problem.
- **Open-mindedness:** Employees who demonstrate critical thinking are open-minded – not afraid to consider opinions and information that differ from their beliefs and assumptions. They listen to colleagues; they can let go of personal biases and recognize that a problem's solution can come from unexpected sources.
- **Problem-solving attitude:** Critical thinkers possess a positive attitude toward problem-solving and look for optimal solutions to issues they've identified and analyzed. They are usually proactive and willing to offer suggestions based on all the information they receive.
- **Communication:** When managers make a decision, they must share it with the rest of the team and other stakeholders. Critical thinkers demonstrate excellent communication skills and can provide supporting arguments and evidence that substantiate the decision to ensure the entire team is on the same page.

Benefits of critical thinking in the workplace

Many workplaces operate at a frantic tempo that reinforces hasty thinking and rushed business decisions, resulting in costly mistakes and blunders. When employees are trained in critical thinking, they learn to slow the pace and gather crucial information before making decisions.

Along with reducing costly errors, critical thinking in the workplace brings the following benefits:

- **Critical thinking improves communication.** When employees think more clearly and aren't swayed by emotion, they communicate better. "If you can think more clearly and better articulate your positions, you can better engage in discussions and make a much more meaningful contribution in your job.

- **Critical thinking boosts emotional intelligence.** It might seem counterintuitive to associate analytical rationality with emotional intelligence. However, team members who possess critical thinking skills are less prone to rash, emotion-driven decisions. Instead, they take time to analyze the situation and make the most informed decision while being mindful and respectful of the emotional and ethical implications.
- **Critical thinking encourages creativity.** Critical thinkers are open to new ideas and perspectives and accumulate a significant amount of information when facing decisions. Because of this, they're more likely to come up with creative solutions. They are also curious and don't shy away from asking open-ended questions.
- **Critical thinking saves time and money.** By encouraging critical thinking in the workplace, you minimize the need for supervision, catch potential problems early, promote independence and initiative, and free managers to focus on other duties. All this helps your company save valuable time and resources.

Teaching critical thinking in the workplace

Experts agree that critical thinking is a teachable skill. Exploring critical thinking training programs and methods to improve your workplace's critical thinking proficiency. Here's a breakdown of how to teach critical thinking in the workplace:

1. **Identify problem areas.** Executives and managers should assess workplace areas most lacking in critical thinking. If mistakes are consistently made, determine whether the issue is a lack of critical thinking or an inherent issue with a team or process. After identifying areas that lack critical thinking, research the type of training best suited to your organization.
2. **Start small.** Employees newly embracing critical thinking might have trouble tackling large issues immediately. Instead, present them with smaller challenges. Start practicing critical thinking as a skill with smaller problems as examples, and then work your way up to larger problems, Lawrence said.
3. **Act preemptively.** Teaching and implementing critical thinking training and methodology takes time and patience. Lawrence emphasized that critical thinking skills are best acquired during a time of calm. It might

feel urgent to seek critical thinking during a crisis, but critical thinking is a challenging skill to learn amid panic and stress. Critical thinking training is best done preemptively so that when a crisis hits, employees will be prepared and critical thinking will come naturally.

4. **Allow sufficient time.** From a managerial perspective, giving employees extra time on projects or problems might feel stressful in the middle of deadlines and executive pressures. But if you want those working for you to engage in critical thinking processes, it's imperative to give them ample time. Allowing employees sufficient time to work through their critical thinking process can save the company time and money in the long run.

Successful critical thinking happens during a crisis, not after.

An example involving restaurants and waitstaff: If a customer has a bad experience at a restaurant, a server using critical thinking skills will be more likely to figure out a solution to save the interaction, such as offering a free appetizer or discount. "This can save the hard-earned customer relationship you spent a lot of marketing dollars to create. This concept is applicable across many business and organizational structures. You should also be aware of signs of a lack of critical thinking. Companies that change strategy rapidly, moving from one thing to the next, are likely not engaging in critical thinking. This is also the case at companies that seem to have good ideas but have trouble executing them. As with many issues in business, company leadership determines how the rest of the organization acts. If leaders have excellent ideas but don't follow critical thinking processes, their team will not buy into those ideas, and the company will suffer. This is why critical thinking skills often accompany positive communication skills. Critical thinking doesn't just help you arrive at the best answer, but at a solution most people embrace. Modeling critical thinking at the top will help the skill trickle down to the rest of the organization, no matter your company's type or size.

When critical thinking is actively implemented in an organization, mistakes are minimized, and operations run more seamlessly. With training, time and patience, critical thinking can become a second-nature skill for employees at all levels of experience and seniority. The money, time and conflict you'll save in the long run are worth the extra effort of implementing critical thinking in your workplace.

Emotional Intelligence

Emotional Intelligence is the ability to recognise and manage your emotions, as well as the emotions of other people in the workplace. Someone needs to hold it together when the workplace erupts, or when negative emotions simmer just below the surface, creating a toxic working environment. A leader with high Emotional Intelligence can also help to foster a workplace culture that doesn't become toxic in the first place. Leaders with high EQ can celebrate team balance and diversity, motivate and influence people as well as make decisions using critical thinking and positively influence strategy.

Using Emotional Intelligence

Successful leadership is about being effective in three ways: leading self, leading others, and leading the organisation.

Leading self: Successful leaders know that they are not perfect. They are aware of their strengths and weaknesses, and strive for continuous improvement. A Chief Executive that does not acknowledge their own flaws or blind spots, who tries to do everything by him- or herself, doesn't learn from mistakes and is unable to delegate, will soon be derailed. If you're self-aware as a leader you can work to overcome your weaknesses either through personal development and learning new skills, or by empowering others and using their skills. Motivation is equally important here. Having goals to work towards, and setting high standards for yourself, means acknowledging that there will be obstacles along the way. As a leader, this means constantly challenging yourself, finding ways round the obstacles, and picking yourself up when things go wrong. And you need self-regulation to manage your emotions as a leader. Leadership is tough. So having the ability to keep calm, deal well with pressure and stay optimistic is vital. Mastering leadership of self requires admitting you're not perfect and striving for improvement.

Leading others: Leaders know that they need other people – after all, leadership doesn't mean a lot without followership. Being personally motivated isn't enough – leaders need to unlock the potential of others. This means understanding what matters to people, what their motivations are and how these motivations relate to the purpose of the organisation. Not everyone is the same which makes social skills are important . Successful leaders understand that they need to be flexible and adaptable, as well as able to read and understand others. You need to spend time with different teams, and not just your direct reports. As a leader you don't have to be the master of all trades, but you do need to be willing to listen, to respect the expertise of others and to change your mind, if it's appropriate. And in this time of change, you need to be able to demonstrate real empathy to undertake the most difficult workplace conversations with tact and sensitivity.

Leading organisations: Successful leaders know how to inspire others. Leadership means being visionary, keeping in mind at all times the bigger picture. Leaders can articulate that big picture to others – and the best leaders help people to see their role in that big picture. They also hold themselves and their organisation accountable to that goal. The goal is what is important, not personal gain or success. Leaders need to build strong relationships with boards, partners, stakeholders and even competitors to reach organisational goals. They demonstrate political astuteness, recognizing that power and influence in organisations does not work in neat hierarchical lines. They ensure success through influencing and by networking. Mastering leadership of organisations requires inspiration, accountability and relationship building.

To develop your leadership skills, you don't need to be a robot and turn your emotions off, but rather to focus on interpersonal and intrapersonal skills. Being an effective leader is about technical skill, strategic thinking and knowledge. Being a great leader also requires emotional intelligence.

Leading With Emotional Intelligence: When organizations go through challenging times like the recent pandemic, employers depend upon employees to help the organization come through strong and equipped for the future. If employees are committed and engaged, they're more productive, which positively impacts organizational profitability. The reverse is also true. When I think back to my manager who lacked emotional intelligence and people skills, I remember a time in my life that included daily stress, dissatisfaction, and lack of engagement from the types of assignments I'm normally passionate about. During that period of my career, my productivity was low. Instead of applying innovation and creativity to my tasks, I was focused on completing my work as quickly as possible putting in my 8 hours and limiting my interactions with my manager just to get a paycheck.

Key Components of Emotional Intelligence

1. **Self-Awareness:** The ability to know emotions, as well as your strengths and weaknesses, and recognize their impact on performance and relationships.
2. **Self-Management:** The ability to control both positive and negative emotions and impulses and be flexible and adaptive as situations warrant.
3. **Social Awareness:** The ability to have empathy for others, navigate politically, and network proactively.
4. **Relationship Management:** The ability to inspire through persuasive communication, motivation, building bonds, and disarming conflict among individuals.

It's also important to understand that all emotion is *functional*. Whether your own behaviors or the actions of others are driving positive or negative emotions, both are impactful in different ways. Before you can apply new practices and strengthen your ability to lead with emotional intelligence, assess your current emotions and consider the outcome you want

- **Positive emotions *broaden*:**

  - Supporting resiliency
  - Improving our thinking
  - Undoing negative emotions
  - Building new skills
  - Creating psychological capital

- **Negative emotions *narrow*:**

  - An indicator of potential threats
  - Calls attention to an issue

○ A mechanism of learning

Oftentimes, our negative emotions are provoked when someone or something presses a "hot button." Hot buttons are people or situations that may irritate you enough to engage in conflict and produce destructive responses. The "hotter" the button, the more likely you may be to experience strong negative emotions, feelings of personal provocation, automatic and impulsive responding, and increased tension.

CHAPTER FIVE

Goal Setting and Getting Things Done

Goal setting is part of our day to day life. We all have experience in setting goals whether they are New Year Resolutions such as to up skill, to be healthier, have financial stability, or goals to meet KPI''s for work to grow professionally, or complete certain tasks in a day. We all set goals regularly from short-term goals to life-altering goals (Everest goals). Goal setting is important because it gives **direction** and **focus.** In the journey of self-leadership, emerging leaders need to invest active time in reflective practices to understand their own thoughts, emotions, and behaviors and be more self-aware before setting their self-leadership goals. This requires them to act with autonomy, initiative, and responsibility and to hold oneself accountable for the goals set. Research has linked goal setting with **higher motivation, self-confidence, autonomy** and **self-esteem** (Locke & Latham, 2002). There is also an established strong connection between goal-setting and success (Matthews, 2015). Therefore, an emerging leader without direction may reach the destination but the ride may be full of uncertainty, bumpy and constantly uphill.

The reality is that most people don't know how to write clear, inspiring goals that serve as a roadmap to success. We need to have short-term goals so that we can make adjustments as we go along. If we keep setting short-term goals, we'll never be able to hit the bigger ones. Our short-term goals should focus on a specific behaviour or habit change, such as doing an extra work out a week, eating healthier, taking a walk after work, etc. We also need to set longer-term goals, such as the next 5 years, 10 years, and even 20 years. It's important to be realistic with our goals. If we don't have long-term goals, we'll never get anywhere. Our long-term goals need to be more general. If we're setting goals, we should be aware of the obstacles we may face. We should also have a plan for overcoming these obstacles. We should also make sure that we're having fun. This is one of the most important things to remember. If we enjoy what we're doing, then we'll keep going. If we don't like it, we won't continue to do it.

Choose the task: The best way to choose a task is to set a goal. Use goals to define to-dos.

Goals are accomplishments. The question isn't, "What do you need to do?" The question is, "What do you need to accomplish?" The goal of exercise is health, for example.

There are two things that make goals useful.

First, decide what matters today by adopting a medium-term perspective. For example, with Friday in mind, what matters on Monday?

The second thing that makes goals useful is a deadline. A goal without a deadline is a dripping faucet that sucks joy out of life.

Move forward with resolve: Deadlines clarify timelines and accelerate results. But don't live with constant stress.

Have you ever met a fulfilled leader who ran around with their hair on fire? Hurry is the enemy of excellence and fulfillment. Don't hurry, but don't lollygag.

Be quick, but don't hurry. This morning was the first time I understood the distinction between being stressed and moving forward with conscious resolve.

Get It done.

Focus on one thing: When you do two meaningful things at the same time, both lose their satisfaction. For example, it's dissatisfying to kiss your spouse and think about mowing the grass at the same time.Thinking about the next thing while doing this thing makes both things irritating.

The secret to focusing on one thing is eliminating distraction.

1. Establish a do not disturb hour with your team.
2. Turn off everything that might distract you.
3. Engage in activities that enhance focus.

Principles for creating successful goals.

- **Clarity.** The goal should clearly state what it is that you want to achieve so that both you and the person you're setting the goal with have a shared understanding of what success looks like. It's also important that you're clear about when this goal needs to be reached.

- **Challenge**. Now that your goal is clear. It's important that it's sufficiently challenging to be motivational for the person you've set it for, for this to be successful, you'll need to work to understand the capabilities and aspirations of your team members, bearing in mind different people will have different levels of capability and ambition.

- **Complexity**. Goals that are overly complex or even contradictory won't support achievement or motivate of your team. However, you work in a complex world in one of the most complex organisational systems in the world where there are a huge number of competing demands that set in the complexity. Creating clear goals with your team members can help motivate them to get things done. Part of a team leader's role is to help their people navigate the complexity of the world we're operating in. The key to preventing goals from becoming overly complex is to maintain an ongoing dialogue. Someone may initially be comfortable with a goal and then find they face issues they didn't expect once they start.

- **Commitment**. It can be tempting when you're first leading a team to see your team members as resources who can help get things done, and therefore you just need to set them their goals and the team will achieve what it needs to. The most productive way to gain commitment to your goals from your team is to actively involve them in setting them in the first place.

- **Feedback**. Once goals have been agreed, it's important that you revisit them with your team members and have an ongoing dialogue and feedback on progress to this goal, without this ongoing dialogue, your team members may not feel comfortable sharing that they've uncovered something which needs to be sorted in order for them to achieve the goal. Also, without feedback, the person will not know if they're doing the right things. Ongoing validation should help maintain and even increase commitment to delivering the goal over time. This can be especially useful when talking about objectives agreed at appraisal time. The more often these goals are revisited and discussed, the more useful they will be to the individual and team success.

Setting Goals Plan

Setting a goal: What do you plan on achieving? What is the best way to get there?

Creating a plan: How are you going to achieve your goal? What steps are you going to take to make this happen?

Monitoring progress: Are you making progress towards achieving your goal? What are you doing to stay on track?

Staying motivated: Is it easy for you to stay motivated to achieve your goal? Are there any obstacles that you need to overcome?

It's very important to understand that setting and achieving goals takes time and effort. It's also important to keep your goals realistic and achievable. What is your goal? What do you want to achieve? What is the best way to get there? What is the best way to make this happen?

Achieving Goals

How can you make this happen? The easiest thing to do when setting a goal is to sit down, write out all of your business goals, and devise a plan. But, it doesn't always work. So, what can you do instead? You can set a goal in a different way. It's like trying to run a marathon with no training or practice. You might be able to dream about running a marathon but, you can't always go out and achieve the final goal. When you've achieved a goal, take the time to enjoy the satisfaction of having done so. Absorb the implications of the goal achievement, and observe the progress that you've made towards other goals.

If the goal was a significant one, reward yourself appropriately. All of this helps you build the self-confidence you deserve.

With the experience of having achieved this goal, review the rest of your goal plans:

- If you achieved the goal too easily, make your next goal harder.
- If the goal took a dispiriting length of time to achieve, make the next goal a little easier.
- If you learned something that would lead you to change other goals, do so.
- If you noticed a deficit in your skills despite achieving the goal, decide whether to set goals to fix this.

Examples of leadership goals: Here are several examples of common leadership goals to help you brainstorm your own:

- Increase team productivity by 20% before the end of the second quarter
- Improve retention rate by the end of the year

- Increase profits by 35% by Financial Year End
- Open three additional branches within five years

Increase team productivity by 20% before the end of the second quarter: This goal sets a specific objective of increasing productivity. It's measured by a rate of 20%, which is often monitored through the delivery of assignments or other projects. Team members only need to increase productivity by a small amount, making it an achievable goal. Since companies often measure team productivity through work due dates or turn-ins, the objective has relevance to current work. The goal includes a due date as well, outlining the end of the second quarter. This adds a time-bound nature to the goal, making it a well-rounded S.M.A.R.T. goal.

Improve retention rate by the end of the year: Even without a specific number or percentage, this goal remains specific enough to meet S.M.A.R.T. criteria. The company measures the goal by comparing the previous year's retention rate to the current one. Improving the retention rate within a year is both achievable and time-bound. It's enough time for any changes to make an impact and sets a clear completion date. Having employees on-site to achieve these goals makes the retention rate relevant as well.

Increase profits by 35% by Year End: Concerning S.M.A.R.T. goals, this goal is specific in nature because it outlines increased profits. It also adds a measurable percentage to consider for reaching and attaining the goal. Increasing profits is relevant for any business in any industry, as this relates to the bottom line and the company's overall survivability. The goal sets an objective due date of June 15, making it time-bound and adding a specific completion date.

Open three additional branches within five years: This goal is specific and sets a goal of three additional branch openings. The quantity of three makes it measurable, and with the given time of five years, it's both attainable and time-bound. Most businesses run on the goals of thriving and growing. For some businesses, this means they want to expand their services by opening more locations. Depending on how much capital the business has, three locations in five years is an attainable goal.

Other goal examples include:

- Improve team communication skills by the end of the year
- Create and implement a series of five coaching initiatives by September
- Improve client retention by 10% by the end of the third quarter

- Reduce employee turnover by 5% in two years
- Increase collaboration efforts through five meetings over the next six months

The Basics of Goal Setting

Types of Goals: There are many types of goals that you can set and even more methods for defining goals and tracking success. Let's review some of the prevailing theories and differences between goal types:

Personal vs Professional Goals: Personal goals are aspirations of how you can strengthen a character trait or change a lifestyle habit. These typically center on fitness, family, education, finances or career. Professional goals focus on growing the business. These might include reducing overhead, increasing market share or improving client retention rates by a certain percentage.

To nurture a forward-thinking culture, encourage employees to set one personal goal that stretches their professional vision, such as earning an industry certification, increasing job performance metrics or improving time management skills.

Company, Team and Individual Goals: Company goals should focus on the handful of initiatives that can make a real difference. These are centered on the why and tie back to the mission and values of the organization. While focused, they are also broad enough to apply to every level of the business. If you don't model it, no one's going to do it," he writes. An effective goal-setting system starts with disciplined thinking at the top, with leaders who invest the time and energy to choose what counts. Team goals tend to be project-based or metric-driven, such as hitting a sales target to drive growth. By leveraging the diverse strengths of each member, team goals have the power to propel us further than when we work individually. This approach also promotes real collaboration and teamwork toward achieving a common goal, which builds trust, unity and pride in the outcome. Successful teams encourage collaboration and provide space for trying new ideas, but they also hold each other accountable for decision making and task completion. Individual goals focus on completing a subset of tasks that support team goals. When each person has the opportunity to shine using their skillset and the freedom to innovate, they finder a deeper meaning in their work. That sense of ownership fosters engagement and passion to do better. Individual goals should also challenge employees to stretch their professional skills, which will ultimately benefit the team and organization as a whole. Individual goals feed into team goals, which in turn support the company goals. All three levels should connect to encourage alignment.

Annual to Daily Goals: Annual goals represent your long-term vision of the things you want to accomplish in the future. These big-picture targets support the company mission and serve as a blueprint for prioritizing the plan of action. This broader scope takes time to reach, so you need to break it down into smaller action steps that you can do right now to achieve your bigger dream. Organizing goals into quarterly, monthly, weekly and daily tasks makes reaching the end goal more manageable and keeps you grounded in the present instead of daydreaming about your ambitions. Meeting those minor milestones not only establishes accountability but also keeps you motivated to power on as well.

Goals vs Tasks: Goals are the guiding directive, pointing us toward the work that needs to be done to fulfill our why. Each goal is specific in identifying the desired outcome, how success will be measured, relevancy to the mission and when it will be completed. Goals are limited in number. The sweet spot appears to be between three and five to keep the brain focused. Tasks are the many action steps we take to achieve those goals. Organizing these hows into daily lists keeps us moving forward and helps us manage time more efficiently. Progress on tasks proves that you are moving closer to making your goals a reality. Items that make it onto your list that do not relate to the overall mission should be delegated or nixed from your to-do list.

Traditional Goal-Setting Frameworks: SMART vs KPI vs OKR: Goal-setting systems give us a framework for defining, organizing and tracking the things we want to achieve. They give us perspective on what is most important and keep us focused on those priorities.

The SMART system, which stands for specific, measurable, achievable, realistic and time-bound, is the most widely used framework for clearly defining a long-term vision. The outline is meant to direct action steps, keep goal-setters motivated and prove the success of the project. A major drawback is that SMART goals emphasize attainable and realistic ideas, which can hold followers back from taking bold action or learning new skills in order to succeed. Key Performance Indicators (KPIs) focus on performance management to gauge progress toward a goal. They are based on a blend of business objectives, departmental targets and data. The measurements have the power to strategically improve operational performance and individual efficiency as well as provide a rubric for analytical decision making. However, KPIs need to be tied to the right metrics to be valuable in nurturing growth. They also tend to focus on the outcome despite the quality. Objectives and Key Results (OKR) is a goal-setting model that has been adopted by some of the world's most successful companies, including Google and the Gates Foundation. The objectives define where you want to go. The key results specify how you are getting there. While transparency and measurability are still stressed, the approach also leaves room for flexibility and higher aspirations. Incentives, reviews and salaries are not based on achieving the goals.

CHAPTER SIX

Improving Mindfulness

Workplace mindfulness is the degree to which individuals are mindful in their work setting. What, then, does it mean to be mindful? Well, like so many constructs in positive psychology, mindfulness is not easily defined. Mindfulness can be described as a 'present-focused consciousness. In other words, a mindful individual is not ruminating about the past or worrying about the future; they are simply "being" in the here and now. Secondly, mindfulness includes paying close attention to both internal and external stimuli. Finally, as well as simply paying attention to stimuli, mindfulness involves doing this in an open and accepting way.

Advantages of the mindful leadership approach

Mindful leadership may sound like a "fluffy" term, but it's quite the opposite. It takes a lot of focus and hard work to develop a skill set around mindfulness. Yet, the efforts and practice pay off. In the thousands of hours I've spent coaching executives and leaders, I've seen that leveraging mindfulness in the workplace brings leaders significant advantages.

The mindful leader has the most power in the room: They may not always be the loudest voice but they are the one paying the closest attention. They keep their inner commentary and reactions at bay. They get present and study what's going on in the room. They don't get caught in pettiness or politics. They rise above and see the bigger picture, noticing solutions that others simply can't perceive. They speak up in moments that matter and, when they do, their voice is respected.

The mindful leader creates high-performing, cohesive teams: The mindful leader's approach to individual and team interactions cultivates a sense of psychological safety and loyalty. The people around the mindful leader want to show up and do their best because they feel cared for, appreciated, and seen for their unique strengths and efforts. They know the mindful leader truly cares about them, which motivates them to continually bring their best to the work.

The mindful leader experiences stressful times in a more peaceful, healthy way: The mindful leader realizes they can actively foster inner peace and well-being as they walk through challenges and focus on business results. Because of the self-mastery they have nurtured, mindful leaders know how to navigate difficulties in a more calm and responsive way.

Many leaders feel they don't have time to work on being mindful because their workload is too big and they have too many demands to deliver on. The irony is that if they were willing to spend a few minutes being mindful each day, they could become better equipped to navigate their professional responsibilities and relationships with greater well-being. That can also create a ripple effect that inspires their direct reports to create better results for themselves, too.

The 5 Cs: traits of the mindful leader

People who practice mindful leadership tend to have these specific common characteristics:

Composure: To be with whatever is happening in a responsive and resilient way. In the midst of challenging situations, the mindful leader stays calm and brings an inner strength knowing that somehow, some way, things are going to work out and there will be a path forward.

Compassion: To see oneself and others with love and kindness rather than with judgment. A mindful leader knows that they are a work in progress with plenty of imperfections and opportunities to improve. The leader is gracious and compassionate to others as they are also working on their own growth. A mindful leader seeks to find the best in others while also encouraging them to step further into their potential.

Connectivity: An understanding of the interconnectedness of all individuals on the team and of all the small thoughts, emotions, and actions that culminate as a result. A mindful leader recognizes that each person is needed, has essential skills and strengths to offer, and plays a vital role in bringing about success.

Curiosity: The ability to hold an open mind and a willingness to release judgment. A mindful leader seeks to understand what is going on rather than jumping immediately to conclusions. The mindful leader asks powerful questions to see new angles and possibilities, and is willing to stay open to a wide range of ideas no matter how different and divergent they seem. A mindful leader makes space for the creativity and perspectives of each person on the team.

Caliber: The ability to harness inner power and awareness to bring energy to work to create remarkable, excellent results in the business environment. A mindful leader is not woo-woo, floating on a cloud somewhere. A mindful leader knows how to get the job done with the highest quality and care possible. Rather than working from reactivity, fear, or the stress of nasty competition, a mindful leader fosters a sense of calm and a confidence in the people on the team so they bring a level of excellence to the work at hand.

Mindful Leadership Is a Must-Have Practice for Leaders

Higher Levels of Emotional Intelligence: It is now widely understood that emotional intelligence skills are essentially, by definition, leadership skills. Different from management skills, leadership skills are about inspiring high levels of performance in team members. And, every competency related to inspiring performance in others falls somewhere under the umbrella of emotional intelligence.

The core competency of emotional intelligence is self-awareness. Because mindfulness training is essentially synonymous with self-awareness training, mindfulness training is a systematic way of developing emotional intelligence. Following this logic, it should be clear that mindfulness training is perhaps the best tool there is for developing higher levels of emotional intelligence. And, as you would expect, there is a growing body of research suggesting that this is indeed the case. Other than the core competency of self-awareness, I believe that the two most critical emotional intelligence competencies are self-regulation and empathy. Self-regulation is what allows you to be free from the grip of unpleasant emotions that would otherwise undermine our productivity and your ability to effectively lead team members. Empathy is, in my opinion, the very essence of the most effective leadership. When you truly understand the legitimate needs of team members and do whatever you can to help team members meet those needs, you build the influence that is the hallmark of highly-effective, inspiring leadership. As you might have guessed, self-regulation and empathy are two well-known benefits of mindfulness training with a large body of supporting research suggesting that mindfulness improves both skills.

More Inspiring, Effective Leadership Presence: Another benefit of self-regulation is that it is a key component having a leadership presence that attracts others to you and inspires greatness and those around you. I think we can all agree that given the choice, we would much rather follow somebody who is calm and collected during a crisis than somebody who is frantic and has completely lost control of his or her emotions. In addition to helping you develop the self-regulation that improves your leadership presence, mindful leadership training also helps you to be more present with people when you are interacting with them. In fact, the foundational practice of mindfulness is learning to recognize when you have become distracted by thinking and allow your awareness to open to include what else is happening right now. Although being present with people may seem like a very minor detail, I believe that such presence is perhaps the most powerful way to demonstrate that you truly care about a person.

You've almost certainly had conversations with people, probably very recently, in which the person you were speaking with seems distracted and is either lost in thought, looking around, or, even worse, interacting with a device like a computer or a smart phone. You know how that feels. It feels as though the person you are speaking with does not care about you. They may want to care about you, but they are clearly not demonstrating care in that moment. Conversely, hopefully you have had an experience in which you were interacting with someone who you hold in high regard, and when that person was interacting with you she or he made you feel as though you were the most important person that she was going to interact with all day. You know how that feels, too. It feels incredible. You feel truly cared for, and you're very likely to do your best to help that person, not because you have to, but because you want to.

Better Decision-Making Skills: Another benefit of self-regulation is that it helps to improve decision-making skills. The more powerful the emotion, and the more caught you are in that emotion, the worse your decisions will be. Because mindfulness is so effective at helping you to regulate emotion and develop the ability to become free from the grip of unpleasant emotions, mindful leadership training can help you to significantly improve your ability to make sound decisions, even during demanding situations.

Better Business Acumen: Business acumen is generally defined as the ability to handle a business situation in a way that leads to a positive outcome. From a purely financial perspective, business acumen is your ability to have a positive impact and the profit and loss statement (P&L).

Over the long term, it has become crystal clear to me that the leadership skills (people skills / emotional intelligence skills) have the greatest impact on the P&L. Senior leaders can develop an incredible strategy, but if team members are cared for by their leaders, even the best strategy will never be executed properly, if it all. That being said, leaders are often put under tremendous pressure to have a positive impact on the P&L in the short term. The practice of mindful leadership, and the self-awareness that it develops, is the surprising bridge between the leadership skills of inspiring greatness in others, and making an immediate and direct impact on the P&L. Nearly every leader knows what they need to do to have a positive impact on the P&L, but very few actually have a consistent, positive impact on the bottom line.

Extensive research conducted by the prestigious Perth Leadership Institute has made it clear that the gap between knowing what to do and actually doing it is created by a common psychological phenomenon called a *cognitive bias*. A cognitive bias causes a person to take a sub optimal, often irrational, course of action. There are various cognitive biases that result in courses of action that have a direct impact on the P&L. The research conducted by the Perth leadership Institute has identified five cognitive biases that correlated very strongly with gross margins, and five cognitive biases that are correlated very strongly with expenses. Almost everyone is affected adversely to varying degrees by most, if not all, of the 10 cognitive biases that impact gross margins and expenses. Theses cognitive biases have been programmed into you based on your genetics and your life experiences up to the present moment.

The good news is that you do not have to be controlled by your cognitive biases. The more refined your self-awareness is the greater freedom you have from the control of those cognitive biases. By systematically training self-awareness, you can systematically train yourself to be less constrained by cognitive biases, and thereby have a significantly better impact on the P&L. Because the cognitive biases that negatively affect the P&L are usually completely unconscious for most people, even a slight improvement in self-awareness can make an immediate impact on financial performance. After completing the assessment, we help participants see which cognitive biases are affecting them most. As soon as they become aware of these subtle aspects of their personality, they often make a significant, positive impact on the P&L within days or weeks of taking the assessment. Soon after taking the assessment and being made aware of their cognitive biases, we have had leaders report back that they made a decision that they would not have made prior to taking the assessment that saved their organization tens of thousands of rupees.

Being More Innovative: The practice of mindful leadership helps boost a leader's ability to innovate, as well as the team's ability to innovate, in several key ways. Mindful leadership can help you to be freer from the cognitive bias that most inhibits innovation, to be more open to failure, and to reduce the fear of failure in team members.

Freedom from the Status Quo Bias: According to the extensive research conducted by the prestigious Perth Leadership Institute, mentioned above, there is a cognitive bias that kills innovation. It's called the *status quo bias.* As its name implies, this bias results in people avoiding doing things that challenge the status quo. The research shows that roughly 90% of leaders are naturally wired to be affected adversely by the status quo bias. It seems that most people are wired to value fitting in with the group over doing things that challenge the majority view of the group.

As you would likely guess, the status quo bias kills innovation because innovation is, essentially, a solution that disrupts the status quo. People who are affected very little by the status quo bias, or not all, are the exact opposite. They tend to thrive on challenging the status quo. This, of course, is great for innovation. However, it's not so good for getting along with others. People who are affected very little by the status quo bias, or not all, often need to work hard to cultivate the people skills necessary for effective leadership. Thus, mindful leadership is helpful for both types of people. For people who are not affected by the status quo bias, the practice helps to develop the essential emotional intelligence skills required to lead well. For people who are affected by the status quo bias, mindfulness helps develop greater freedom from the effects of the bias, which can dramatically improve a leader's ability to innovate.

Openness to Failure: Many people tend to think of innovation is something that happens in a vacuum. They envision a person who sits around thinking of the next great idea, and then "bam" it just comes to them. While this does happen from time to time this is by far the exception and not the rule. Generally speaking, innovation is something that happens as the result of building a minimum viable solution and testing that solution with people who will actually use it. This is followed by getting feedback from actual users on the solution and then going back and making changes as necessary to ensure that the solution is adding the most value possible for the end user. This is why one of the key principles for innovation at Google, arguably one of the most innovative companies in the world, is to "Launch early and iterate often" This iterative approach requires an openness, and even a willingness to fail. In fact, another common attribute of innovative teams is that they are not only are tolerant of failure, they actually expect it and even demand it. The faster you can fail, the more quickly you can get to the solution that's going to add significant value for the user. The practice of mindfulness can help improve your tolerance for failure in a couple ways. First, a benefit of the practice is greater freedom from fear. The practice of mindfulness allows you to have less fear in general, and to recover from fear more quickly when it does arise. By having greater freedom from fear in general, you are less likely to be adversely affected by the fear of failure. When you are not adversely affected by the fear of failure, you are much more likely to try things that could end up iterating into an innovative solution that adds tremendous value for the end user of the solution. Second, the practice of mindfulness is, by nature of its difficulty, the practice of failure. If you've been practicing for more than 5 minutes, you already know that the ability to remain mindfully self-aware is incredibly elusive.

Removal of Fear: Because the practice of mindful leadership develops emotional intelligence competencies as well as the qualities of kindness and compassion and generosity, a mindful leader is much more likely to create a team culture where people are not afraid to take calculated risks and try new things. By removing fear from the workplace, mindful leaders can increase the team's capacity for innovation tremendously.

Improved Strategic Thinking: You have likely noticed that when you're caught up in the day-to-day minutiae it's very hard to think at the strategic level. Leaders often intentionally square away time, by taking retreats or carving out moments in the day to step away from day-to-day activities, so that they can gain the highly prized "30,000-foot view," as it is often called.

Better Team Building Skills: One of the more direct examples of how having high levels of self-awareness helps you to be more effective as a leader is in terms of understanding your own strengths and weaknesses. This ability to understand your strengths and where you have room for growth is important both in terms of understanding how you can continue to develop as a leader as well as building the most effective teams. In order to have a highly effective team, you must have a very clear and objective view of where your strengths lie and where you are not as strong. One of your primary jobs as a leader is to find people who are very strong where you are weak so that the team as a whole has few or no weaknesses. As we will discuss further below, mindful leadership training is the systematic development of objective self-awareness. With consistent practice, your ability to see yourself with complete objectivity and clarity grows increasingly stronger.

Freedom from the Ego: Perhaps the most important benefit of practicing mindful leadership is that it gradually increases your freedom from the control of your ego. Although being free from the ego may not be so easily seen as a having a tangible impact on organizational outcomes as the benefits mentioned above, I believe that this is the most important factor of leadership development. The freer you become from the control of the ego the easier it is for you to plan an act in ways that benefit the entire team or organization without being biased by your own short-term self-interest. This is absolutely essential for leaders. A successful leader must be able to put her short-term self-interest aside for the benefit of the team organization. This is not to say that you don't take care of your own legitimate needs for well-being. Rather, you move away from always prioritizing your needs first and more towards having a balanced approach to meeting your needs and the needs of the organization and, when necessary in the short term, putting your own needs aside for a brief time and sacrificing yourself for the benefit of others.

Integrity that Inspires True Greatness In Others: Unless you are an incredibly rare, and perhaps perfect human being, you've probably noticed that there is often a gap between who you would like to be, and who you actually are. A simple definition of integrity is having no gap between who you want to be (or who you state you are) and who you *actually are*. The less often there is a gap between who you aspire to be and who you actually are, the more others will perceive you as a person of integrity and the more you will see yourself as a person of integrity. The practice of mindful leadership plays an essential role in allowing you to have such integrity. Whenever you are mindfully self-aware, you see whatever internal reaction arises within you with third-person objectivity. As a result, there is gap created between stimulus, the internal reaction, and the external reaction or response. When you see your internal reaction with this type of third-person objectivity, you are completely free from having to act on it. If the internal reaction is one that is not in alignment with who you aspire to be, i.e. your core values, then you can simply not act on it and instead choose to do something that is in alignment with your core values. Thus, mindfulness allows you to live with integrity in a given moment and increases the likelihood that you will live with integrity in future moments as well.

Living with high levels of integrity is essential for living a fulfilling life, and it is also a key component of inspiring team members. Leaders of high character, who live with integrity, can inspire followers much more readily than other leaders. And living with high levels of integrity is not just good for your team. It's good for the world. The world is replete with smart, talented people. What the world needs more than ever, especially during times of division, is more wise people of great character who demonstrate that taking the high road is always the more inspiring and effective path.

CHAPTER SEVEN

Improving Self Awareness

Self-awareness is the ability to monitor your own emotions and reactions. It allows you to know your strengths, weaknesses, triggers, motivators and other characteristics. Being self-aware means that you take a deeper look at your emotions, why you feel a certain way, and how your sentiments could turn into reactions. Practicing self-awareness allows you to better react to situations or people who might set you off, which is a healthy skill to cultivate – especially as a leader. When you're aware of your emotions and how you handle them, you're better equipped to process and work through them, avoiding unnecessary conflict. This will also help you set a good example for your team and make them more comfortable approaching you with questions or concerns. Even if you're not where you want to be as a leader, developing self-awareness and acknowledging areas you need to work on is the first step.

Without self-awareness, leaders can appear arrogant. If you cannot be personable, or know when you are crossing a line, how can you lead a company? The need for self-awareness extends to other business situations, too. Think about how crucial self-awareness is in giving sales pitches or handling feedback, for instance; if you are not aware of how you will react or do not have a way to prevent a negative reaction, you could get yourself in trouble. Self-awareness is also helpful for presentations. Many people get nervous when delivering pitches, speeches or even notes at a meeting. Self-awareness can help. If you use too many filler words during presentations, for example, practice your presentation and have someone clap every time you use a word you want to avoid. If you tend to sway or pace around while presenting, limit your ability to move by sitting down at the table with your client or by using a podium.

Self-awareness skills: In addition to being aware of your own emotions, self-awareness involves knowing how you will react to others. Self-awareness keeps us grounded, attuned and focused," said Campbell in her book. "When leaders are grounded, they are able to be efficient and deliberate in staying on task and being attuned to those around them. Leaders who have the ability to control their minds and emotions help to guide those around them to develop their own self-knowledge and success.

These are some important self-awareness skills:

- **Empathy:** When you fine-tune your self-awareness abilities, you will become more empathetic thanks to heightened emotional intelligence.
- **Adaptability:** If you know how you will react, you could avoid a tough situation by taking a walk or just engaging in a few deep breaths.
- **Confidence:** By accepting and even embracing your flaws, needs and strengths, you will increase your ability to be vulnerable, which allows for stronger relationships in the workplace. Maintaining confidence is key to success.
- **Mindfulness:** When you're self-aware, you become more mindful of the present moment, allowing yourself to take situations as they happen rather than dwelling on the past or projecting into the future.
- **Patience:** While your immediate reaction might be to scold an employee for a mistake or let your frustrations out on your team, self-awareness will help you practice patience, even in the face of conflict.
- **Kindness:** This is achievable when you put aside your own feelings to support another person. Even if you're having a bad day, being self-aware and realizing your workers are also human beings with similar struggles can help you be more sympathetic.

Become more self-aware: Learning to be aware of yourself isn't always easy, but it can help you become a more effective leader.

1. **Keep an open mind.** When you are able to regulate your own emotional world, you can be more attuned to others' emotions. To be a successful leader, you need to be curious about new people and all they have to offer. This shows that you can be a team player and don't need to be Number One all the time. The more open you are to others, the more creative an entrepreneur you will become.
2. **Be mindful of your strengths and weaknesses.** Self-aware individuals know their strengths and weaknesses and can work from that space. Being mindful of this means that you know when to reach out for

assistance and when you can handle a situation on your own.

3. **Stay focused.** An important part of being a leader is making connections, but you can't do that if you're distracted. Train yourself to focus for long periods of time without getting sucked into social media, emails or other small distractions to improve your productivity.

4. **Set boundaries.** A leader needs to put strong limits in place. Be warm toward others, but say no when it's needed. Be serious about your work and your passions, and keep your boundaries firm to maintain the integrity of your goals and the work you put into them.

5. **Know your emotional triggers.** Self-aware individuals can identify their emotions as they are happening. Don't repress your emotions or deny their causes; instead, bend and flex with them, and fully process them before communicating with others.

6. **Embrace your intuition.** Successful people learn to trust their instincts in decision-making and take the risks associated with those choices. Your instincts are based on the survival of the fittest and the need to succeed. They will tell you what to do next, so learn to trust your intuition.

7. **Practice self-discipline.** Good leaders tend to be disciplined in every area of their lives. This trait provides them with the enduring focus necessary for strong leadership.

8. **Consider how your actions affect others.** We often act without thinking first, focusing only on our own needs. While self-awareness requires acknowledging your emotions, you also need to identify how you handle those feelings and how any subsequent actions impact those around you. Being more considerate of others will help you navigate difficult situations.

9. **Apologize when necessary.** Mistakes happen, but being self-aware will help you recognize when your slip-ups require apologies. Maybe you lashed out at your staff, or perhaps you've been difficult to reach lately. Whatever your mistake was, saying you're sorry (and meaning it) and then changing your behavior is the best way to move forward.

10. **Ask for feedback.** While the concept of being self-aware is to understand yourself without input from others, it takes courage (and self-awareness) to ask for honest employee feedback. Doing this acknowledges your natural biases toward yourself (which we all have), and helps you gain a more objective view.

Organizational Benefits of Self-aware Leadership: By becoming more self-aware, and subsequently recognizing their strengths, weaknesses and hidden biases, leaders gain the trust of their team members and increase their own credibility. Additionally, a culture of self-awareness advances learning and development (L&D) by promoting the value of continuous growth and development. When people are self-aware, they can put their tensions on the table, and no one gets hurt, because we're trying to improve. So, we have this culture of continuous improvement, and we don't take things personally. In addition to helping leaders develop professionally, self-awareness also helps them have a positive impact on the business. For one, teams led by self-aware leaders are less likely to experience internal conflict. "In the end, a culture of self-awareness creates a space where people can address their tensions in a more open and less friction-based way.

Striving for More: Self-aware leaders strive for more than individual success. They want to use their expertise and passion to enact change on a large scale. In order to make a lasting difference, however, leaders must first use their sense of self-awareness to objectively determine areas they need to improve. "We have to have that clarity about what is and what is not true and be willing to embrace it and accept it and look at it as a resource to make our lives greater, and make the world greater which, again, is our whole responsibility. At its core, self-awareness offers leaders far more than another tool for success. It helps them remember why they wanted to become leaders in the first place. It helps them discover, and live, the impact they want to have, not just on their team members or even on their organizations but on the world. And, that is a leader worth following.

CHAPTER EIGHT

Managing Workplace Anxiety

It is crucial to be proactive regarding mental health issues in this fast-paced world. There is a call for companies to embrace vulnerability in their staff, listen actively, communicate openly, and lead with compassion. And businesses can help pave the way for mental health awareness and support when managing workplace stress and anxiety.

Raise awareness about mental health: Businesses can't deliver mental health support if they don't understand it. And so, leaders must have solid knowledge about workplace stress and anxiety to support their teams.

The following resources are a fantastic way to equip senior management with the knowledge they need to support others with their mental health struggles:

- APT-USE provides a variety of accredited mental health training courses delivered by world-class mental health experts.
- Mental Health First Aid at Work is an excellent source of key information about mental health and workplace stress and provides effective workshops for organizations.

Encourage communication from the top down: Executives and managers must lead by example to encourage positive change within the workplace. It is up to company leaders to empower those with mental health difficulties. And thus, it is essential to start from the top down to equip senior management with good communication skills. If you practice what you preach and lead by example, you will experience more success in encouraging employees to communicate openly with one another. Many executives who struggle with mental health difficulties bring their struggles to the workplace and often spend their days feeling anxious, depressed, or isolated. Therefore, good communication is essential for the success of your business and the wellness of your team. Leaders and managers should build a company culture that encourages open discussions about mental health concerns.

Provide wellness strategies and training: To effectively support employees struggling with workplace stress and anxiety, management must have the right training to drive positive change. Training leaders and managers on wellness strategies, spotting mental health symptoms in others, and listening and providing support are great ways to kick start mental health programs in organizations. Such initiatives are great for promoting mental health conversations at work. Most importantly, they help management understand employees' needs and concerns related to workplace stress.

Ask for feedback and make changes: Measuring the results of your efforts is one of the best ways to show your employees you care about their mental health. Taking the time to collect employee feedback through in-person meetings and anonymous surveys is vital for tackling workplace stress and anxiety.

Ask your team the following questions about the new changes in supporting staff with anxiety and workplace stress:

- How safe do they feel about sharing their mental health issues with management?
- Are there any changes to their workload or work environment that would help relieve feelings of workplace stress and anxiety in their day-to-day?
- Is there anything else they would like support with?

You can also send out a similar survey for leaders to analyze how successful your training has been and whether leaders feel fully equipped in their role or not. By requesting feedback and implementing the changes based on the same, your organization will be taking proactive steps to drive positive change for your business and your employees' health.

Looking after your team

1. Much stress comes from being overloaded. If you need your staff to put in more hours for a specific project, then make sure it is for a set, acceptable length of time and always show you appreciate the extra effort. Ensure that staff take breaks throughout the day and take all their

holiday entitlement.

2. Encourage employees to push themselves to the next level but know and accept with respect if they simply don't have the skills, where training is needed, as well at times what they are simply not well-suited to.

3. Be flexible to different workers' requirements such as working from home and being open to part-time work; some of the best workers want to work part time and keeping their skills in-house is vital.

4. Be quick to identify if a team member has mental health issues of any sort or is simply going through a difficult period and offer your support in the best way you can.

5. Involve your staff in key decisions by listening to opinions from a diverse cross-section. Give respect and time to your team and be open to constructive criticism or suggestions where possible. Actively listen to reduce stress.

Reducing your own stress

1. Identify the signals of stress as early as possible such as anxiety, depression, sleepless nights, overwhelmed and irritability, as well as physical signs such as high blood pressure, heartburn and muscle tension. Know when things are out of balance, if stress has turned into distress, take action to prevent it from taking over. Talk to someone whether it's a colleague, friend or family member.

2. Manage external pressures. During a stressful work period, concentrate on one task at a time and prioritise your work instead of trying to do everything at once. Multi-tasking is a myth. When we try to do more than one thing at a time we are in actual fact switching rapidly between tasks. This is costly in terms of efficiency because we lose precious time with each switch and costly in terms of our stress levels. Concentrate on one thing at a time and get it done.

3. When you are in the moment of high stress, know when to take time out. Sometimes it is best to allow your mind time to recover and recuperate. Just going for a ten-minute walk outside can really help.

4. Accept that there are periods of stress at work when you have to put in longer hours that may be acceptable as long as it doesn't dominate your life. Make sure you find ways to have downtime, relax, disconnect and recharge.

5. Remember that small amounts of stress for short periods can help us be more creative in finding solutions, develop resilience and even build confidence if we succeed at resolving any issues.

Causes work anxiety

Generally speaking, there are four kinds of anxiety at work: **performance anxiety, impostor syndrome, urgency,** and **generalized anxiety.** Here's how they differ from one another:

Performance anxiety: If you're generally pretty comfortable at work or around your colleagues, but get nervous when you have a project or presentation to complete, you likely have performance anxiety. This is a short-lived phenomenon that tends to disappear after you've successfully completed the project (or even sometimes, in the middle of it when you start to build confidence).

Impostor syndrome: Imposter syndrome makes us feel as if we don't deserve the level of success we currently have. People that deal with imposter syndrome tend to second-guess themselves and dismiss compliments. They constantly worry that someone will find out they're not qualified for their role — despite evidence to the contrary.

Urgency: Some jobs require quick decision making or crisis management. These roles can be inherently stressful. Particularly when someone's decisions can mean the difference between life and death (for example, emergency medical staff) the body reacts by triggering the stress response. Ideally, this response dissipates when the immediate threat is gone. However, over time the result of chronic workplace stress and trauma can accumulate, leading to anxiety disorders.

Effects of work anxiety

Workplace anxiety can leave you feeling awful. Because we spend so much of our time at work or thinking about work, anxiety can quickly make its way into every area of your life. Here are some effects of untreated anxiety in the workplace:

Loss of self-esteem: For many of us, our jobs reflect part of how we see ourselves. Doing well at work is important to us because not only does it provide financial security, it affirms how we see ourselves. When our identity at work is compromised, it tends to impact our ability to feel positively about ourselves.

Reduced self-efficacy: Self-efficacy is our faith in ourselves and our ability to produce results. A key part of building self-efficacy is whether or not you feel positively about the task at hand. When you feel good, you're better able to take on and succeed at new challenges. When you don't feel good, it becomes harder to stay resilient in the face of work-related stress.

Physical illness and pain: The body doesn't function well under chronic stress. Near-constant anxiety can cause — or exacerbate — a number of health issues. Some stress-related ailments include migraines, heart disease, gastrointestinal upset, and sleep disturbance. Stress can also compromise immune function, making you more susceptible to illness and colds. If you're experiencing stress-related ailments, reach out to a professional for medical advice.

Poor performance: Anxiety makes it difficult to focus, organize our time, and meet deadlines. When we don't feel comfortable asking for help at work, it makes it harder to get support or ask clarifying questions on projects. A sudden change in an employee's performance or participation is often a warning sign of underlying anxiety.

Tips for managing workplace anxiety

Get enough sleep: Stress at work can cause a vicious cycle when it comes to sleep. Stress can cause you to stay awake at night, and this lack of sleep will leave you vulnerable to even more stress. Being well-rested will make managing your emotions and coping with stresses much easier. To set yourself up for a better night's sleep.

Talk to an attentive listener: Talking face-to-face with good listener can help calm your nervous system and relieve stress. The goal isn't to have the person "fix" your problems, it's just an opportunity to offload.

Eat well: Diet can have a profound effect on your mood and sense of wellbeing, with processed meats, packaged meals and sugary snacks all being strongly linked to today's higher rates of depression, stress, bipolar disorder and anxiety. Foods rich in zinc, magnesium, omga-3 fatty acids, probiotics, and B vitamins have been found to reduce anxiety.

Create a balanced schedule: Those who find themselves very stressed at work often might be giving too much value to what happens in the workplace. While there's nothing wrong with trying hard and being ambitious, try to remember that the purpose of work is to enable you to live a great life. If you can learn to change your priorities so that work is not your only priority, you may find that your workplace anxiety will decrease. Analyse your schedule, responsibilities, and daily tasks and try to find some kind of healthy balance. All work and no play is a recipe for a burnout, so be sure to include time for work, family life, social activities, solitary pursuits, daily duties and downtime.

Leave earlier in the morning: Rushing to your desk every morning will leave you feeling flustered and add to your stress levels. Try leaving 15 minutes earlier each morning and slow down your commute. Leaving a little earlier will let you ease into your day. This may also mean that you miss the worst part of rush hour, meaning you will have a more relaxed journey.

Learn when to say no and when to delegate: Over-committing yourself to many projects might mean you simply have too much on your plate. Firstly, understand when to say no, and then find ways to delegate tasks you don't need to do yourself. Let go of the desire to control everything and realise you can't do it all on your own. It's okay to ask for help.

Break projects up and prioritise: If a large project seems overwhelming, break it up into smaller tasks and create a step-by-step plan. Focus on the most manageable and important tasks first, and before you know it there will be light at the end of the tunnel. You could also try getting the most unpleasant of tasks done first so that the rest of the project seems more enjoyable.

Improve your emotional intelligence: Emotional intelligence is just as important as intellectual ability, if not more so. It has four major components: self-awareness, self-management, social-awareness, and relationship management. Taking steps to improve these components, such as looking for ways to inspire, influence, and connect with others in your workplace can help distress your work environment. Recognising your own emotions and the impact they have will also help the situation. Laugh more, resolve conflict quickly, and factor in your feelings and those of your colleagues when making decisions.

Break bad habits: Workplace anxiety can be the result of some of your own undoings, such as working in a messy environment, always requiring perfection, and trying to control the uncontrollable. Turning these habits around can make an impact on your overall anxiety levels. Understand that no project is ever going to be perfect, and that it doesn't have to be. File work straight away and keep your desk clear. Look for the good in your work instead of the bad and accept the aspects that are out of your control.

Find the "off" button: Carrying your work with you wherever you go can be extremely exhausting, so be sure to hit the "off" switch now and again. Turn your phones and gadgets off between 7PM and 7AM, and refrain from checking emails at lunch. Take your sandwich away from your desk and focus on simply eating or chatting with friends.

Exercise: Exercise is vital for maintaining mental fitness and is known to reduce stress and anxiety. Physical activity produces endorphins that act as natural mood-boosters and help promote sleep, which in turn reduces stress. A brisk walk or other simply physical activity can deliver several hours of relief from anxiety, and regular exercise has been shown to have long-term effects. Try aiming for three hours a week of moderate exercise or two hours of rigorous exercise a week. Look for consistency rather than perfection, by including 20 minutes of exercise into each day.

Know when to open up: If you feel that your workload is unreasonable or your deadlines are too rushed, talk to your supervisor. Engage them in the process and explain your concerns so that if you miss a deadline, they are aware of the reasons in advance. Telling your boss about your stress and anxiety is a personal decision, and one only you can make. Always seek professional advice if you think you may be suffering from an anxiety disorder.

Tips for Facing Your Return to Work Anxiety

- **Acknowledge your Feelings.** With the unavoidable change and uncertainly associated with the return to work, it's important to expect some level of anxiety and not be surprised by it. Anxiety is normal when faced with these types of changes, and it's not an indication that something is bad or unsafe for you. Keep in mind that it will dissipate in time and there are resources to help you work through it.
- **Plan Ahead.** While you can't anticipate how everything will go when you return, there are many things within your control, and simple planning ahead can help regain a sense of control. Is there a pre-pandemic routine that you envision changing, and if so, how will you plan ahead to adapt to this new routine? This could be a shift from eating lunch out most days to instead meal prepping each weekend so you have something to bring with you for lunch each day.
- **Focus on the Positive.** While we're hard-wired as humans to pay more attention to the negative, it's important to take a step back and remember what we miss about working on campus. Was it a quick lunchtime walk along the Charles, or maybe catching up with colleagues each morning? Remembering what previously brought you joy each day can help make the transition easier.
- **Be Considerate and Aware of Others.** One thing we've learned from the pandemic is that everyone's comfort and safety level is different, and the

transition will affect us all in very different ways. Furthermore, please be sensitive and aware of the unique stress of employees with marginalized identities. Many people with marginalized identities have enjoyed less of a need to conform to majority culture appearance standards and greater protection from the trauma of micro aggressions. Returning to in-person work for many brings increased anxiety and exposure to micro aggressions.

Reach out for Help. Despite best efforts, you might still need help, and that's ok. There are resources available on campus to help you through this transition. We encourage you to keep an honest and open line of communication with your manager, as well as to reach out to the Faculty Staff Assistance Office for free and confidential counseling.

CHAPTER NINE

Personal Productivity

Personal productivity is efficiently accomplishing tasks that bring you closer to your goals while maintaining balance across key areas of your life. Being more productive on an individual level can mean different things depending on what matters to you — whether it's nurturing social relationships, being more healthy, or increasing one's income. In the end, it's all about prioritizing the right things in order to achieve your goals without succumbing to burnout. Why set goals in the first place? Well, when you set a long-term goal for yourself, you have something to look forward to every day. Finishing your to-do list is no longer just a source of fleeting satisfaction but a part of a bigger picture. In fact, the sense of purpose we derive from goal setting has been linked to greater well-being, and is even considered "the cornerstone of happiness, flow, optimal experience, and a life well-lived. Working on your personal productivity won't be easy but each challenge you face is an opportunity for self-improvement. The distractions you face and mistakes you make will teach you to gain better control over your time, energy, and attention. Despite all the possible obstacles, the mere fact of having a North Star will motivate you to keep pushing forward.

There's a simple equation for measuring productivity: The amount of value you create divided by the number of hours you work. A person with high productivity will create the same amount of value for an organization in a shorter time or create a more significant amount of value in the same amount of time. The problem is, it's hard to measure personal productivity this way as you won't always have a clear understanding of the value you create. This is especially true if your work doesn't involve creating a physical product, making output harder to measure. So it might be easier to think about productivity in terms of the total number of productive hours you have on an average day or week. A productive hour is one where you get stuff done - where you feel you can concentrate on a task and complete it, free from distractions. Many of us feel more productive at certain times of the day or week than others. And distractions range from sudden meetings and phone calls to chat notifications to having too many small or odd jobs getting in the way - all of which prevent you from getting the "big stuff" done.

When it comes to measuring your personal productivity, you might want to ask yourself questions like:

How much time do you have on an average day to focus on one specific task?

If your calendar is full of admin blocks or if you tend to work on two or more projects simultaneously, this may affect your productivity.

How many meetings do you usually have in a day?

Do you regularly find yourself juggling multiple tasks or unrealistic deadlines?

If this often happens, it suggests you need to reassess your approach to work – do you need to delegate more?

Are you able to take regular breaks, including a lunch break?

Breaks are essential for maintaining focus, so you need to carve out time to step away from the screen.

How to Improve Personal Productivity

If you want your team to be more productive, you need to pay attention to your personal productivity too and the only way to do that is to manage your work and life better while protecting yourself from stress and fatigue. The rest of this article will introduce you to different types of apps and productivity systems that'll help you optimize your personal productivity.

Best Personal Productivity Tools

Personal task management software: Ever had a long day you couldn't wait to end only to have trouble sleeping at night? This can happen if you have many unfinished tasks occupying your mental space. Keeping a dedicated to-do list app is a simple but life-changing way to silence that mental chatter and ensure that you don't forget anything. A great to-do list app lets you capture tasks quickly from multiple devices, set due dates, and organize tasks based on different areas in your life. There are hundreds of task management apps right now that looking for the perfect one can leave you frustrated. Before you start your search, it's important to list down your current needs and evaluate your prospects' features so you can choose the best one that suits your workflow.

Calendar app: While a task manager keeps track of what you need to do, a calendar app gives you the discipline to actually get them done. If you don't plan your day in advance, you'll get sucked into unforeseen distractions. Scheduling your tasks will help you stick to a routine so you don't have to go through feelings of uncertainty which often leads to procrastination. Find a good calendar app that integrates with productivity apps you're already using. It doesn't have to be full of advanced features as long as it's easy to use and share with people you collaborate with. When scheduling your tasks, be careful not to overdo it. Your calendar should only be used for time-sensitive tasks, events, meetings, and appointments. Leave a little time for yourself to unwind and find inspiration.

Note taking app: It's tough to beat pen and paper for taking notes quickly but if you want to store them somewhere you won't forget, note-taking apps are your best bet. Notes apps don't just capture knowledge and ideas; they help you organize them in a way that makes sense to your workflow so you don't spend a lot of time looking for them later. They provide structure to your project planning and knowledge management so you stay organized no matter what kind of work you do. There are so many different ways to take and organize notes that it feels like there's a new note-taking app popping up every other day. Whatever app you choose, just make sure it covers fundamental functions like cross-platform support, offline access, usability, and the ability to store images and other types of media. The best note-taking app for you really depends on how you learn and how you keep track of the different types of information you consume. Find something that's flexible enough to fit various use cases whether that's taking meeting notes or conducting research.

Focus app: Having trouble focusing nowadays? It's not entirely your fault — not when the modern workplace is full of distractions that are beyond your control. Luckily, there's a whole genre of productivity apps designed to help you solve this very problem. Focus apps work by blocking distracting websites or by providing a digital workspace conducive to single-tasking. Some apps generate white noise, ambient sounds, or functional music that trigger a state of flow. Other apps lock you out of specified websites and apps while making it hard to disable them and there are those that set a focus timer and encourage you to stay on task. Depending on how easily distracted you are, it might be worth considering an all-in-one tool that combines all of these functions.

Time management app: Knowing how to manage your time well will help you accomplish your tasks faster and reduce stress. If you're serious about improving your productivity, understanding exactly where your time is spent is a good place to start. There are several types of time management apps out there, but the best ones not only track the hours you work but also provide detailed reports about tasks you completed and how much time you spent on email, meetings, social media, and other websites. With that, you can set a goal and adjust your work style and schedule to accommodate more time for focused work.

Habit tracker: We've talked about how goals provide a clear direction in your life but cultivating daily habits is what pushes you to make real progress. You can build a habit out of something positive (e.g. exercising more) or eliminate a bad one. The longer you stick to your habits, the more motivated you'll feel as you work towards your goals. While there are task management tools flexible enough to let you create your own habit-tracking system within them, there's another type of app focused on doing just that. Habit tracker apps let you set streak goals, earn rewards, or export your data so you can better understand how you're progressing.

Automation apps: On a typical workday, you'll most likely rely on multiple tools to do your best work, but spending too much time copy-pasting information from one app to another can distract you from what's important. That's where workflow automation comes in. Automation or integration apps connect your disparate tools so that your data can move freely between them. These days, you can automate pretty much any time-consuming task without learning how to code. For example, you can use Pleexy to automatically send emails, notes, and tasks from other apps to your preferred task manager. This way, you don't have to manually check for updates in different places and you'll always have a centralized view of your projects at work and in life.

Pomodoro Method: If you can't focus on a single task for sustained periods, try incorporating the Pomodoro Method into your workflow. Here's how it works: you work on something for 25 minutes, take a 5-minute break, and repeat. After four Pomodoro sessions, you take a longer break for 15 minutes. When you break down a large task into smaller steps, it's easier to get started. The frequent breaks in between will replenish your mental focus and motivation throughout the day. Working in short bursts will also give you some added pressure to get the job done within the given time period. Because each session is allotted for just one task, you'll train your mind to be better at resisting distractions.

Eat The Frog: Eat The Frog is a simple productivity method that's useful for anyone who tends to procrastinate or has trouble deciding what to work on first. The frog refers to your most intimidating task which you're most likely to put off. By doing it first thing in the morning when you have the most energy and willpower, you can get it out of your way earlier and set yourself up for a productive day. If you have more than one frog, tackle the most challenging one first. Do this every day and you'll keep making progress on high-impact work. Plus, the rewarding feeling you'll get when you accomplish what you set out to do will motivate you to keep going.

Getting Things Done: The Getting Things Done (GTD) methodology created by David Allen is arguably the most famous productivity system right now. It rests on the premise that anything that captures your attention should be recorded in an external system. Otherwise, they'll pile up and keep pestering you in the back of your mind. After capturing a task, idea, or important piece of information in your trusted task management system, you'll review them later and decide what to do with each one, whether you should act on it immediately, schedule it for later, or file it away. It's imperative that you review your to-do lists regularly to keep them organized and avoid creating an unmanageable backlog of work. With this system in place, you'll never forget to do something and when you need to rest, you can do so with a clear mind.

Don't Break the Chain: Personal productivity entails diligence in key areas of your life where you've set a goal for yourself. To do that, you must make it a habit to show up consistently until your goal feels more attainable. With the Don't Break the Chain productivity method, you're encouraged to do one thing every day that brings you closer to your goal. It's so simple that you only need a physical calendar and a pen to get started, but you can always turn to digital habit trackers if you want. For each day that you accomplish your daily goal, mark your calendar with an X until you see a chain of X's. The only thing you need to do is to make sure you don't break your streak. Over time, the habits you build will become second nature to you, like exercising or meditating.

Steps to Improve Your Personal Productivity

- Write down all your goals and break them into small and manageable steps.

- Incorporate productivity systems to achieve your goals and hold yourself accountable. Use the daily planner to start.
- Eliminate distractions as much as possible.
- Create a tech stack of productivity tools and online meeting tools either for yourself or for your team. Use these to automate tasks, jobs, and to roadmap your day.

Don't forget to give yourself a pat at the back when you achieve your goals and reward yourself! You deserve it.

It's hard to maximize personal productivity given today's busy culture. But the right strategies and tools will make it easier for you to balance the demands of your professional and personal life. You don't have to stick to a certain system religiously because each one can be adjusted to accommodate your needs and lifestyle. The important thing is that you're taking actual steps to work more effectively while making time for the things that matter.

Public Speaking

Most leaders today are often evaluated by their abilities to speak effectively. If you listen to effective leaders, one of the skills they possess is their ability to speak in public. Becoming a better speaker is a learned skill and an art. Many of today's leaders were not good public speakers earlier in their careers. Unlike reading and writing, public speaking is not one of those basic skills we are taught during our school years. To those with no public-speaking experience, often they feel their only option is to write out their entire speech word-for-word and memorize it. Of course, that's not an easy task, and it's time-consuming. Furthermore, most of us don't write like we speak. So when we try to speak the words we wrote, it feels — and sounds — awkward. As a result, many of us fail at our first public-speaking assignment, which leaves us with a lot of negative feelings about public speaking. As we get older we avoid public speaking altogether due to this first negative experience. The good news is, we can all become better speakers with the right tools and guidance.

Few short tips on becoming a better speaker (and leader):

- **NEVER MEMORIZE YOUR SPEECH OR PRESENTATION**
  Instead of memorizing your talk, think about the key points or concepts you want to discuss and just talk about them conversationally.
- **USE CONVERSATIONAL LANGUAGE**
  Learn to just have a conversation with your audience. When we approach speaking as a performance, we are worrying more about what the audience is thinking and not focusing on just having a conversation.
- **PRACTICE AND REHEARSE**
  Most people do not rehearse or practice their presentation. Practice your presentation out loud. Record your presentation and play it back and take notes. Listen to what you said and how you said it, make changes

and adjustments, and then repractice and rerecord the presentation until you feel comfortable with what you are saying and how you are saying it.

- **FOCUS ON YOUR MESSAGE**

  Do not focus on the audience. Focus on your message and how to effectively deliver that message. Remember, the audience wants you to succeed. If you find yourself thinking about yourself, how you sound, how you look, etc., you are taking away the focus on your message and your nervousness increases.

- **TAKE A PUBLIC SPEAKING CLASS**

  The quickest way to improve your public speaking is to take a public speaking class. Read about how to do presentations and how to improve your public speaking skills. Work with a professional who can give you the proper guidance and help to improve and practice what you are taught. Becoming a confident public speaker is achieved only by focused effort and a lot a practice. The good news is your payoff will come quickly, you'll have fun along the way, and the confidence you develop will improve virtually all areas of your life.

Reasons why it is important for a leader to also be a public speaker:

Unite people for a single goal: Inspiring speakers know the motive of their speech even before they start speaking. Their voice, tonality, and body language are all directed towards uniting the crowd and making them believe in a single goal. If you don't exude confidence while talking, you won't be able to convince your crowd to believe in your message. All your leadership skills will be of no use if you can't unite your team to work together.

Drive positive changes: Do you want to bring about a major change in your team? If yes, you need to gather your team at one place and deliver a convincing speech about the changes you want to initiate. Your team members are more likely to be influenced by you when you speak in front of them as compared to when you send them an email that contains the changes you have in mind.

Connect with your people: A leader who is committed to the success of his team members is more likely to win them over than someone who only wants to see himself succeed. An easy way to show your people you care is by being honest with them and taking them into confidence. However, if you're unsure of how to communicate with your team members in team meetings, you'll never be able to establish a connection with them.

Make people follow you: A leader without followers is similar to a guitar without its strings – useless. A leader needs to be confident that his people recognize him and his authority. As your team members become familiar with you standing in front of them and delivering a speech, your visibility and authority steadily increases.

Public speaking allows you, as a leader, to show your team what you are thinking and what direction you want to take: they will see you as not only an actual leader but as a thought leader. A leader isn't just someone, who states what they want to be done and waits for people to do it. A leader is someone who motivates positive action, who inspires innovation and growth, who sets a set of goals for a group of people and helps them to find the path to their mutual success. There's no question that the only way that any of these ideals get accomplished is through clear communication — both as an active listener and speaker. If you want people to follow you, you have to communicate effectively and clearly what followers should do. Powerful leadership comes from knowing what matters to you. Powerful presentations come from expressing this effectively. Learning public speaking is the one thing that can change your life forever and it's best to master the skill at a young age. A person who is able to skillfully express himself or herself as an orator, especially early in life, is more likely to foster better friendships and relationships and build a larger network of collaborators. If you want to grow as a leader and persuade people to invest in your ideas, you must also invest in your public speaking skills. Words are extremely powerful, because you can use them to move people to act on your ideas. In fact, the public speaking champion believes that brilliant ideas are worth nothing until they are brought to life with the power of your words.

Public Speaking Types of Speeches

Here are different types of public speaking formats, each with a different purpose. Let's look at 3 of them that applies most to organization leaders:

Speaking to Inform: Speaking to inform means that you have information you wish to relate to your audience. The primary purpose of this format is to help the audience gain knowledge of a particular process, place, person or event. As a leader, you would be using this because the information you are providing is either to be accountable to your team, or to aid them in their work.

Speaking to Persuade: Speaking to persuade means that you are trying to influence your audience to think and act in a certain way. The primary purpose is of this is to align your team member's goals with the organizational goals, or to get their buy-in for a particular decision you are making.

Speaking to Inspire: Personally, speaking to inspire is the best kind of public speaking because of its power to motivate and encourage your team. I find that this is also the easiest form of speaking because you don't have to have length preparation; you simply speak sincerely from your heart.

CHAPTER ELEVEN

Social Intelligence

Individuals with social intelligence can sense how other people feel, know intuitively what to say in social situations, and seem self-assured, even in a larger crowd. You might think of these folk as having "people skills," but what they truly possess is social intelligence. The theory of social intelligence was first brought to the forefront by American psychologist Edward Thorndike in 1920. He defined it as, "The ability to understand and manage men and women and boys and girls, to act wisely in human relations." No one is born socially intelligent. Instead, it involves a set of skills that an individual learns over time.

People who are socially intelligent display core traits that help them communicate and connect with others.

- **Effective Listening:** A person who possesses social intelligence doesn't listen merely to respond but truly pays attention to what a person is saying. The other folks in the conversation walk away feeling like they were understood and that they made a connection.
- **Conversational Skills:** Have you ever seen someone "work the room?" They have conversational skills that enable them to carry on a discussion with practically anybody. They're tactful, appropriate, humorous and sincere in these conversations, and they remember details about people that allow the dialogue to be more meaningful.[2]
- **Reputation Management:** Socially intelligent people consider the impression that they make on other people. Considered one of the most complex elements of social intelligence, managing a reputation requires careful balance—a person must thoughtfully create an impression on another person while still being authentic.
- **Lack of Arguing:** Someone with social intelligence understands that arguing or proving a point by making another person feel bad isn't the

way to go. They don't outright reject another person's ideas, but rather listen to them with an open mind—even when it's not an idea that they personally agree with.

Develop Social Intelligence

While some people may seem to develop social intelligence without really trying, others have to work to develop it. Luckily, certain strategies can help a person build social skills. These tactics can help you develop social intelligence:

- **Pay close attention to what (and who) is around you.** Socially intelligent people are observant and pay attention to subtle social cues from those around them. If you think that someone in your life has strong people skills, watch how they interact with others.
- **Work on increasing your emotional intelligence.** Although similar to social intelligence, emotional intelligence is more about how you control your own emotions and how you empathize with others. It requires recognizing when you're experiencing an emotion which will help you recognize that emotion in others—and regulating them appropriately. An emotionally intelligent person can recognize and control negative feelings, such as frustration or anger, when in a social setting.
- **Respect cultural differences.** More than that, seek out cultural differences so you can understand them. Although most people learn people skills from their family, friends and the community surrounding them, a socially intelligent person understands that others might have different responses and customs based on their upbringing.
- **Practice active listening.** Develop your social intelligence by working on your communication skills—which requires active listening.Don't interrupt. Take time to think about what someone else is saying before you respond. Listen to the inflections in what others say, which can give you clues to what they really mean.
- **Appreciate the important people in your life.** Socially intelligent people have deep relationships with people who are meaningful to them. Pay attention to the emotions of your spouse and children, friends, co-workers, and other peers. If you ignore the closest people in your life, you're missing the cues on how to connect with them.

Ways to Improve Social Intelligence

Do you want to improve your social intelligence? Here are great ideas with which to get started with.

Listen well and pay attention: Practice active listening so that you can fully engage and communicate with others. Life is often fast paced, with many distractions both digital and otherwise. It is natural to want to respond to that text message that pops up on your phone immediately, even when you're in the middle of a face-to-face conversation. Give people your full attention when speaking with them. People like to feel heard, and it will help you develop worthwhile relationships.

Watch out for body language: Often, people's body language will tell us a great deal about how they are feeling, even if they aren't saying so. Try to tune in to what the other person is saying 'physically. In the same way, be aware of your own body language and how you are presenting yourself. If you slouch and appear physically uninterested during a conversation, it may make the speaker lose confidence in what they are saying, resulting in a negative interaction.

Show that you care: If you sense that someone is upset, or if someone tells you they are going through some difficulties, show them you truly care. Displaying empathy for others can help you connect at a more meaningful level.

Fostering Social Intelligence in the Workplace

Having a socially intelligent workforce may be more important than you think. At work, we need to co-exist and cooperate with others with whom we may or may not typically socialize with. For those in management or leadership positions, the ability to connect with and motivate a team can be key to the success of a business or institution. In other words effective leadership relies on the ability to inspire others through meaningful connection and the ability to foster positive feelings in the people whose cooperation they need. In fact, there is a subset of mirror neurons whose sole purpose is the detection of other people's laughter and smiles. This, in turn, prompts your own laughter or smile. A leader who smiles and uses humor can set these specialized neurons to work, encouraging a relaxed interaction and positive emotions in others. In fact, studies show that top-performing leaders elicit laughter from their subordinates three times more often than mid-performing leaders

Key elements of social intelligence

Verbal Fluency and Conversational Skills. You can easily spot someone with lots of SI at a party or social gathering because he or she knows how to "work the room." The highly socially intelligent person can carry on conversations with a wide variety of people, and is tactful and appropriate in what is said. Combined, these represent what are called "social expressiveness skills."

Knowledge of Social Roles, Rules, and Scripts. Socially intelligent individuals learn how to play various social roles. They are also well versed in the informal rules, or "norms," that govern social interaction. In other words, they "know how to play the game" of social interaction. As a result, they come off as socially sophisticated and wise.

Effective Listening Skills. Socially intelligent persons are great listeners. As a result, others come away from an interaction with an SI person feeling as if they had a good "connection" with him or her.

Understanding What Makes Other People Tick. Great people watchers, individuals high in social intelligence attune themselves to what others are saying, and how they are behaving, in order to try to "read" what the other person is thinking or feeling. Understanding emotions is part of Emotional Intelligence, and Social Intelligence and Emotional Intelligence are correlated — people who are especially skilled are high on both.

Role Playing and Social Self-Efficacy. The socially intelligent person knows how to play different social roles — allowing him or her to feel comfortable with all types of people. As a result, the SI individual feels socially self-confident and effective — what psychologists call "social self-efficacy."

Impression Management Skills. Persons with SI are concerned with the impression they are making on others. They engage in what I call the "Dangerous Art of Impression Management," which is a delicate balance between managing and controlling the image you portray to others and being reasonably "authentic" and letting others see the true self. This is perhaps the most complex element of social intelligence.

How can you develop social intelligence: It takes effort and hard work? Begin by paying more attention to the social world around you. Work on becoming a better speaker or conversationalist. Networking organizations, or speaking groups, such as Toastmasters, are good at helping develop basic communication skills. Work on becoming a more effective listener, through what is called "active listening" where you reflect back what you believe the speaker said in order to ensure clear understanding. Most importantly, study social situations and your own behavior. Learn from your social successes and failures.

CHAPTER TWELVE

Social Learning

Social learning is a concept automatically and instinctively applied by humans throughout their lives, which they implement from childhood in order to find their place in the world and society. Fundamental beliefs and worldviews, such as gender roles, religion, political views, and self-worth, are initially shaped through social learning. This happens by observing how those around us react to different opinions.

Social learning is learning by observing other people with the goal of adapting one's behaviour in social contexts. People typically don't adopt worldviews that make the most logical sense, but we are influenced to adopt behaviour that earns the least amount of criticism in our unique environment. It is human nature to want to be accepted by others, so we automatically observe how others behave and what the consequences are in order to adapt our behaviour. With social learning, we use this technique to adopt the behaviours with which another person has been successful in order to achieve the desired result. While social learning is usually associated with learning specific content, it is actually a process that we naturally use subconsciously every day of our lives. The term social here refers to the fact that one questions and adjusts one's behaviours based on observation of other people in a social setting to achieve a desired outcome. Motivation, work ethic, and learning techniques are examples of observed behaviours you can imitate to achieve a desired result. Behaviours learned through social environments can have a circular impact and inspire others in the same social setting.

Why does social learning matter? : In traditional learning environments, most people recall only 10% of the information taught within 72 hours. Consider the impact that lack of knowledge retention could have on your organization. For example, a salesperson may have trouble recalling the lessons they learned from an annual sales kickoff event by the next week. That could cost the sale and have a negative impact on your bottom line. Not good, right? Social learning helps organizations reverse these kinds of potential outcomes. After all, one of the concept's main goals is to drive knowledge retention. Instead of relying on traditional models with low recollection rates, social learning encourages learning in working environments and allows learners to pull knowledge from experts within the organizations instead of having knowledge pushed on them (like a formal learning system would).

There are several reasons to adopt social learning in the workplace:

- **Shorter orientation times for new hires:** It can take up to 2 years before an employee is "fully productive." For some employees, they may require as long as 6 months to simply feel fully comfortable in their new position. Social learning accelerates this process by acclimating new hires to their co-workers and internal subject matter experts quickly, encouraging them to feel comfortable asking questions and creating connections across the entire organization more effectively.
- **It promotes constructivism:** Constructivism is a standard that promotes learning as an active and constructive process in which learners become teachers. It assists in creating a workforce full of stakeholders that are engaged with their training as a result of informally training their peers.
- **It improves communication in the workplace:** Communication should be clear in every workplace, at every level of the organization. It can be easy to lose meaning over email and other electronic communications, increasing the need for face-to-face interactions. Social learning facilitates collaboration organically, especially in an e-learning environment, in which insights are shared and valued across the entire organization.

Principles of social learning
The behaviorist formulated four principles of social learning.

1. Attention: We can't learn if we aren't focused on the task at hand. If we believe something as being novel or different, it's more likely that that concept becomes the focus of our attention. Social contexts reinforce these perceptions.

2. Retention: Humans learn by internalizing information. We recall learned information when we need to respond to a situation similar to the situation in which we first learned that information.

3. Reproduction: We reproduce previously learned information (behavior, skills, knowledge) when required. Practice through mental and physical rehearsal generally improves responses.

4. Motivation: We need motivation to do anything. More often than not, humans are motivated by someone else being rewarded or punished for something they have said or done. This generally motivates us to do, or avoid doing, the same thing.

Components of Social Learning

Observation: Social learning works by observing the behaviour of other people. The consequences of specific situational actions are observed, then that behaviour is mirrored depending on the outcome of the consequence. In this way, people learn which behaviours are socially acceptable and which behaviours are usually criticised. Observational learning allows people to adapt and approach situations more confidently quickly.

Assessment: Next, we assess whether the observed person's behaviour fits our personality and whether the results and reactions of others are desirable. If we decide that we would like to be praised and recognised for something, we analyse how the observed person came to this result. There is often not enough data to know on which factors the desired reaction depends. Therefore, it is often necessary to observe similar situations repeatedly to develop a better understanding.

Imitation: After observation and assessment of a particular behaviour, imitation follows to achieve the desired consequence. Imitation can only happen within our personal limitations, e.g. physical traits, characteristics, and experiences. In most cases, the consequences of a behaviour depend on several factors. The views of the other person, place, time, one's character, the situation, everything can play a role in how others react to something. Therefore, it usually takes repeated positive feedback for a behaviour to become a habit, but it only takes a little criticism to avoid it in the future.

Identification: A large part of social learning is based on the idea that people want to identify with others and their achievements, or earn the appreciation of those role models. As it is understood in social learning, identification is comparable to the Freudian notion of the Oedipus complex. A part of this concept is about internalizing or adopting the behaviours of other people.

While the term imitation refers to only a single aspect, identification is about several learned behaviours coming together. Imitations, such as language use, attitude, habits, or views, help people achieve feeling similar to role models. It is important to emphasize that while social learning is based on imitating another person's behaviour, it can have completely different consequences. People are individuals, and so are the results of behaviour. Social learning should serve as a way to help you see if others' successful behaviours work for you as well. However, it should not become a direct comparison of results. It is about trying new techniques, habits, and behaviours for yourself, but you should not expect to get the exact same results as your role model. Social learning is not about becoming a different person or modifying your personality to be more like someone else. It is about improving your skills and thus becoming better than you were yesterday.

Social learning theory

- Learning is not purely behavioral, but instead a cognitive process that takes place in a social context. It's why learners prefer to learn in groups, in which an interchange of knowledge and perspective creates new knowledge personal to individual learners.
- Learning occurs by observing a behavior and then observing the consequences of putting those behaviors into action.
- Learning involves observation, extraction of information from those observations, and making decisions based on the expected output or performance of that behavior. Therefore, it would suggest that learning can occur without any observable changes in behavior.
- Reinforcement plays a significant role in learning but is not entirely responsible for it.
- Learners are not passive recipients of information, but instead, cognition, environment, and behavior all influence each other (reciprocal determinism).

While social learning has its roots in the beginnings of human history, it's only now becoming so popular (especially among corporations) because technology has caught up to the point that its benefits are measurable and able to address common concerns related to its efficacy in the workplace. Social learning technologies now have a huge impact on a number of core enterprise processes, including recruiting, onboarding, training, and developing talent. The best thing for organizations is that the results are quickly measurable, as social technologies have a direct and obvious effect on performance.

As more learning opportunities present themselves in the workplace, a collaborative social learning environment establishes opportunities for troubleshooting, problem-solving, design implementation, research and development, and innovation to find answers, even in the absence of a coach or mentor. In an ideal world, a result of this would be an improvement in workplace productivity, while those within the organization constantly develop.

Adopting social learning in the workplace

It's important to remember that social learning is not necessarily about learning in groups, but rather learning through the example of others. With that in mind, here are a few ways social learning can be introduced to the workplace.

FAQs and forums: Create a simple place (or forum) where employees can ask questions and get answers from within the organization to promote a social culture of collaborative learning.

Organization wikis: An inter-organizational wikipedia is a great source of knowledge, especially for new employees or those who aren't familiar with every facet of the organization. Allow subject matter experts to edit wiki content as it is critical to keep information relevant and up-to-date, and encourage users to pull that information whenever they need it.

Leverage expert knowledge: There are undoubtedly people within your organization that have questions and people with the expertise to answer those questions. Create communication channels where experts can use their knowledge to help others and encourage users and other experts to rate answers, making sure that only the best ones are used (and shared).

Gamification and rewards: You can't force people to learn, but you can give them the right tools and incentives to make sure they don't waste opportunities. Gamification and rewards can help create these incentives. Gamification gives learning administrators a way to track learner progress and performance. Well-performing users and experts who regularly offer their knowledge can be rewarded to incentivize participation.

Make social learning effective in the workplace

Today, organizations that learn together, grow together.

Social learning is arguably the most widely used learning strategy among adult learners. By sharing performance experiences, lessons learned, solutions to business challenges, and the creative ideas needed to solve them, learners are able to gain a wider spectrum of knowledge within a social learning environment.

Here are just a few things you can do to make social learning effective in your organization.

Make onboarding faster (and easier): New employees can kickstart their learning process by getting answers to questions from their peers at any time, starting from day one. Better than that, scheduled training can happen anytime, so your new people don't have to wait for it to start being productive.

Ask questions and get answers at the point of need: Asking questions and testing solutions on actual problems in real time is one of the most effective ways to learn a procedure.

Get them to contribute (even if someone's a passive learner): Not everyone's over the moon about the idea of having to get in front of their peers to ask a question. With virtual channels, you can give those who are a little shyer a way to contribute to the conversation without making them step out of their comfort zone.

Learn at your own speed: Not everyone learns at the same pace. If answers to particular questions are available online at any time, they can be reviewed over and over again until the concept is retained effectively.

Create a Community of Coaches (or just take part in whatever capacity you want): People in the organization are experts in their own particular area. Everyone should be encouraged to take part in a discussion, at any level. Encourage employees to engage freely and develop knowledge that makes them experts across various facets of the business.

Show off your talent: iI the organization is creating expertise, that knowledge should be shared. Make note of contributions by senior team members, experts, or other role models that can be facilitated and encouraged by an environment that rewards top performances with measurable recognition—doing so can go a long way in growing talent within the organization.

CHAPTER THIRTEEN

Stress Management

Leaders in any workplace are burdened with huge responsibilities of guiding their teams towards the achievement of professional success. They also need to take care of the welfare of their team members, while still maintaining their own professional capabilities. These tough workloads may exert pressure on their mental well-being. However, these leaders need to cope with these pressures efficiently, and to minimize the harms caused by stress on their physical and mental health. They need to learn the effective techniques of stress management and resilience building from experts in these areas, which are highly beneficial for both of them and therefore their team members.

Ways Leadership Stress Affects You: From conflict management to decision-making and people development, a long list of task-related and interpersonal workplace demands contribute to rumination and leadership stress. As you experience your body's physiological responses to these stressful demands, you may assume that you understand what it means for stress to have an "adverse impact on your health." But some of leadership stress's most damaging side effects go unnoticed in the short term and only manifest themselves over the long term.

If you consistently feel stressed, you're probably doing a lot of rumination, which affects your body in 3 main ways:

- **Ruminating affects your health by releasing 2 hormones into your system.** The first hormone is *adrenaline*, which causes your heart to speed up. As your heart pumps faster, blood hits the artery walls, and plaque builds up. Over time, that can lead to an increased risk of a heart attack. The second is the steroid hormone, *cortisol*. In order to produce cortisol, your body puts white blood cell production on hold. Without adequate white blood cell production, your immune system is suppressed, and you're more susceptible to illness.

- **Stress affects your attitude.** People who frequently ruminate because they're stressed often verbalize their thoughts. Verbal rumination not only perpetuates the negative emotions they've associated with their experiences, but it also affects the attitude and resilience of those around them. Negative self-talk is particularly unhelpful in uncertain times.
- **Rumination affects your productivity.** It's hard to focus if you're spending the majority of your time ruminating. As a result, you're often less productive at work.

According to our research, leaders most often turn to sensory pursuits as a form of stress management. These pursuits range from activities that provide healthy physical stimulation, like running, to risky behaviors, such as punching a wall in frustration or overeating. Because leaders rely so heavily on sensory pursuits, it's important to find go-to activities, such as exercising or listening to music, that relieve your stress while also contributing to your overall health. In addition to drawing on positive sensory pursuits, leaders can take the following actions to counter the harmful effects of stress.

Recognize your stress signals: Learn to pay attention to your body's responses to leadership stress. What triggers a feeling of stress, and what are your physiological responses? Do you feel your heart rate going up? Do you get hot? Do you clench your jaw? The sooner that you recognize your body going into stress mode, the sooner you can take action to manage it.

Incorporate health and a proper diet into your schedule: A healthy sensory pursuit, exercise helps leaders reduce their anxiety, improve their sleep, and boost their immunity from colds and the flu. Exercise and dietary changes can support brain health but are more sustainable when they're incorporated slowly. Begin by adding more fruits and vegetables into your diet, while reducing added sugars, fats, and sodium. Then make a commitment to exercising at least 30 minutes, twice a week.

Maintain boundaries between home and work life: This starts by setting expectations. Share your work hours and preferred communication channels with your team. Control as much as you can of your schedule to live with intention both at work and at home.

Enlist a coach to help you stay on track: A coach can support you and help you uncover ways to boost your energy and maximize your time. Together, you can determine which of your responsibilities are essential, and which ones are patterns of behavior you've created that may not be necessary.

Create your personal board of directors: Make sure you have a support group in place that is helping you positively cope with stress and leadership. This diverse group can provide different types of support and should include your peers, your boss, a family member, and a trusted friend. Be clear about your stress-management goals, and ask your advisers for help staying on track.

Practice the art of recovery: Athletes have long understood that pushing oneself hard at 100% capacity, 100% of the time results in little or no long-term performance gains. Make sure that throughout your day, you give yourself frequent breaks. Get up from your desk and walk around, or get outside for some fresh air. After an extended push on a project or assignment, take a vacation, or at least unplug while at home. Learn about other practices for recovery from overwork.

Focus your attention on the present: When you find yourself ruminating, connect with your 5 senses, and then come back into the present. Refocus your attention by asking yourself: What can I control right now?

The link between power and stress: On a scale from 1 to 7, how much stress do you currently feel in your job? A score of 1 would mean you are *as cool as a cucumber*, while a score of 7 would mean you are like a volcano ready to erupt. How do you think your power affects your perceived level of stress? On the one hand, the ever-increasing demands and pressure to meet the expectations that often come with powerful positions can cause more stress. On the other hand, one can also argue that because leaders have access to and control over more resources, they experience a higher sense of control, which *in fine* translates into less stress. Indeed, research indicates that power reduces stress. However, if that power comes under threat (for example when your job is no longer secure) the story can be quite different.

Power and stress relate to your leadership

Possessing and experiencing power is associated with several positive effects (e.g. less distrust in the organization and work stress, but more action, optimism, abstract thinking and goal-directed behavior). However, when it is destabilized, it can have adverse consequences, such as more distrust in the organization and work stress... but not only:

- **Risk taking**: Powerful people are deemed more likely to take greater risks and resort to risky negotiation tactics. Lack of attention to potential dangers and the search for rewards are the two main elements that encourage powerful people to engage in risky behaviors. However, Professor Jordan's lab experiments showed that only powerful people who are in an unstable situation and have a low tolerance to stress engage in more risky behaviors.
- **Power sharing**: A power threat can also affect how much a leader will allow their subordinates to influence/participate in decision making. Interestingly, the negative relationship observed between a power threat and power sharing (as reported by subordinates) is driven by distrust in the organization. In other words, a leader who feels that they risk losing their power is less likely to share their power because of a lack of trust in people in the organization.
- **Transformational leadership**: Finally, a power threat also influences how leaders inspire and motivate their troops. Research suggests that the greater the threat to power, the less a leader applies transformational leadership (i.e. leading by doing, inspiring, fostering collaboration among work groups, etc.). In other words, when a leader feels their power is threatened, they go into a sort of "survivor mode" and effectively stop leading. This, however, is completely explained by work stress, which is not the case for directive leadership.

So, when you feel that your power is threatened, it not only increases your stress level, it also affects how you behave as a leader.

Stress is contagious, so it is important to prevent your own stress from cascading to your team to safeguard their performance and well-being. One way to do this is by being mindful of the physical and psychological resources that you are providing your subordinates with during unstable times. Are they being asked to do too much with too little? Are they aware of the uncertainty around them? And if so, how can you reduce their stress? Being able and willing to see yourself through others' eyes is a key leadership attribute. And while being authentic with your team might help you lead effectively in general, it can backfire when it comes to sharing your stress. You need to find a balance between showing your true self and avoiding the negative effects that this could entail if you contaminate your team with your stress. Your subordinates are unlikely to perceive you as disingenuous if you refrain from sharing something for their good. That said, you do need someone with whom you can share your stress and fears within the organization. This is where your trust cabinet is even more important. Overall, maintaining stability within your team and reducing uncertainty can then be crucial in a stressful context.

Manage your energy

Preventing stress can be difficult. It is possible to do so to some extent by managing your own energy. A person's total energy comes from four dimensions, referred to as batteries:

- **Physical** (general health and vitality);
- **Mental** (ability to process information, clarity and focus);
- **Emotional** (resilience and emotional self-regulation);
- **Spiritual** (values and purpose in life).

These four batteries are interrelated. Everyone has a battery that depletes faster than the others, and one that charges faster. This may vary depending on the context. For example, imagine you've been focusing all day on writing a report. At last, you are pleased with it and send it off to your boss, who congratulates you on a job well done. As you have been seated all day, your physical battery would still be charged, but your mental one may be depleted from an extended period of concentration. Your emotional and spiritual batteries may be boosted by your sense of achievement and your boss's appraisal. People are often good at managing one battery and not another. Think of energy as water that evolves and fluctuates. You cannot be fully charged all the time; and of course, you would not want all your batteries to be depleted for any length of time. You need to find your happy fluctuation zone by optimizing your energy within your specific constraints. To do so, you first need to observe the levels of your different batteries and how they are impacted in different situations. It is important to learn to recognize the early signs of a battery depletion or overcharge (e.g. are you smiling less, feeling tense, have headaches?) and which of your batteries recharge or drain fastest. Then, identify two key points to better manage those batteries. For example, is a person, an activity or a memory sapping your energy? When you lack sleep, does it trigger a domino effect? What could you do to avoid these situations?

- Power lowers stress, but its instability increases stress. It is also important to be self-aware of your power and how it impacts your behaviors and subordinates.

- Stress is contagious and can quickly cascade to your team. Being fully authentic might not always be the best option. Reducing uncertainty and maintaining stability are critical to reduce stress within your team.
- Being able to anticipate bad events, when relevant, reduces uncertainty and stress. But over-anticipating hypothetical events that may never occur can increase stress levels.
- Your energy level can be divided into four components: physical, mental, emotional and spiritual. Learning what your chargers and drainers are and taking action to avoid excessive battery leakage will help you optimize your energy.
- There are plenty of tools available to help you better manage your energy. It's just a matter of finding those that suit you best and using them.
- Remember, stress is a choice! As the Dalai Lama says: "If a problem is fixable, if a situation is such that you can do something about it, then there is no need to worry. If it's not fixable, then there is no help in worrying. There is no benefit in worrying whatsoever.

The benefits of stress management for leaders in all areas of work life include:

- **Better motivation for teams** – When the leaders learn to manage their stress effectively, they find themselves more capable of inspiring their team members to reach their potential and do better work. These leaders can in turn, help their juniors to be stress-free and boost their morale in the workplace.
- **Boosts productivity at work** – The productivity in a stress-free team is sure to be enhanced mainly due to the relaxed temperament of the leader of that team. It makes sense therefore that the leader should be a role model for their team, and be as stress-free as possible to expect better productivity from his team members.
- **Improves relationship with the team** – The stress-free leaders find themselves more capable of handling work-life integration, which improves the conditions of both their personal and professional lives. The balanced and friendly – though not over familiar - nature of a leader encourages their subordinates to share all their challenges with the leader and other team members, thus making the team stress-free as

well. The leader also earns more respect from team members, improving relationships with them all.

- **Ability to solve all issues** – A good leader with a stress-free mind can easily spot any signs of trouble in his team, and quickly and effectively solve these issues as they arise. Since the techniques used in managing stress are also very beneficial to creating emotional management, when used 'in the moment', the mind of the leader can immediately become clear to handle any challenges in the workplace. This may also help them to objectively handle any bullying and/or unethical practices that may be occurring in the team with firmer yet fairer hands, without reacting too harshly or personally with the concerned team members.

- **Retain the team size** – When the team leader is guiding his team in most positive manner, it is less likely that team members will want to leave the team. As training team members is such an expensive investment, it provides a greater return on investment when the same team, happy and efficient team can continue to work synergistically to yield the best results for all projects undertaken. On the contrary, disgruntled and unsatisfied team members may lose necessary focus as they are constantly on the look-out for better work options, and therefore leave the team at the first available chance.

- **Improves speaking and writing abilities** – A stress-free leader communicates more freely and effectively with his team members and superiors, thus improving the entire working environment. The leader is also able to make observations for performance appraisals more objectively and quickly, which makes him a better leader and saves him time and energy in the process.

The best leaders in both large corporations and small to medium sized enterprises, are invariably more highly regarded for their emotional intelligence rather than that of their intellect.

Such simple stress management tips as taking short walks or meditation breaks at work, daily exercise, setting and keeping personal and team goals and being the role model for their team by living a more healthy and balanced lifestyle, not only brings out the very best in the leaders but in every member of their team as well.

Taking Initiative

Successful leaders do not wait for someone to tell them what to do. They think on their feet and take appropriate action, are proactive rather than reactive, and appear flexible, confident and courageous. They help their teams and organisations to innovate, progress and overcome competition, and they spot and take advantage of opportunities that others pass by. Are you doing more or less than what's expected of you at work? When you see a potential problem, do you bring it up? Do you get excited about ways your team can improve? Do you share your ideas or keep them to yourself? If you're doing more and speaking up, it sounds like you're trying to become a team member who takes the initiative in the workplace. What is initiative and what does it mean to take it: Taking initiative means thinking proactively about tasks— not just to check them off a list, but to get them done well. It's about going the extra mile on the basic tasks you're assigned, thinking through complications, and taking on work before someone asks you to.

Taking initiative means noticing opportunities and taking action: Another word for taking initiative might be "ownership." At BetterUp, for example, "radical ownership" means that we are fully responsible for our work and that we welcome the opportunity to learn from it and improve when it doesn't go well. If you're the type of employee who takes responsibility and pride in their work, it will benefit both your team and your own career goals. Plus, you will likely experience more satisfaction in your job. Your employees mirror what they see in their supervisor because they understand that to be approved behavior. When they see that your method works, they gain confidence in the ability to do their job and become less resistant to new rules or procedures. The courage, enthusiasm, and energy with which you take any initiative, big or small, motivates them to work on the same frequency. Along with the improvement of work processes, 79% of employees say they have/will quit a job due to insufficient appreciation from their supervisors proving that even if you're a natural born leader, leadership training is crucial for employee retention.

'Leadership Essentials: Taking Initiative' provides an overview of why initiative is essential for leadership capability and includes 'Top Tips' on how you can become a better leader by taking the initiative.

Not everyone is comfortable with taking the initiative, or even knows how to do so. It is something that is developed mentally and takes strength to do. Some individuals have a bounded rationality. These individuals are unable to see past what they currently know. They cannot see the benefits of stepping up. Typically, the individual has never thought about it. Also, individuals do not take the initiative due to a lack of capability. Outside their general knowledge, some individuals do not possess the expertise to take the initiative for a more difficult task. Execution over innovation is also another popular reason that individuals do not take initiative. These individuals only focus on their own work, and do not have concern for any new tasks. Finally, some individuals are too busy to take the initiative. There is already too much on their plate, and they physically and mentally cannot process anymore work.

Internal causes for lack of initiative: When someone is new in their workplace, they might not want to rock the boat. They may fear speaking up or misspeaking, self-doubt, and a lack of self-confidence. Even experienced employees can feel like they don't know enough to step up. Team members may also view taking the initiative as extra work and not be interested in the benefits. If you notice that you tend to shy away from being a proactive team member, ask yourself why. Try to make purposeful contributions that matter to you — either because of the outcomes or because of the personal career benefit — when you can.

External causes for lack of initiative: The environment you work in and those around you can impact how proactive you are. People who constantly complain and don't respect and appreciate their team members often stop people from taking the initiative. If nobody has team spirit or long-term visions of their work, it's harder to encourage people to be proactive. Occasionally, your supervisors might be threatened or put off by your willingness to work harder or your desire to grow and succeed. Remember that this isn't on you. You shouldn't hinder your growth opportunities just because others don't want to see you excel. It is worth checking in honestly with yourself to confirm that you are delivering on your current responsibilities as expected.

Overcome a lack of initiative: Whatever the reasons stopping you from taking the initiative, you can overcome them. Like any other obstacle or aspect you want to improve, it takes time and effort. Seek input (and moral support for trying new things) from a few trusted co-workers or even friends outside of work. Objective guidance from a coach or mentor can help, too.

Taking initiative doesn't have to mean always going it alone or chasing the spotlight. But it does mean being willing to take the first steps.

- **Internal Inhibitors:** It's all about building confidence and experience and finding your voice. You have helpful skills and perspectives to offer in your workplace. Asking questions when you're confused doesn't make you look bad or lazy. It shows that you're engaged and willing to be a team player and overcome your challenges.
- **External inhibitors:** Use your confidence to speak up and be willing to lead. If a team member or supervisor seems to be throwing up obstacles or putting you down, you need to address it.

Consider whether they are trying to guide you or put the brakes on your plan because they have more context — in which case, seek their input or enlist them in your efforts.

Tips for taking initiative and being a good leader:

Boost confidence, Give honest feedback. Let employees know when they are doing things right. Express satisfaction and give honest feedback to boost employee confidence and overall company morale. This helps build open communication culture.

Take Accountability. Although something might not be your fault, when you're overseeing a group of people it is still your responsibility. Taking responsibility and being open to suggestions on how to better prepare your team to prevent future mistakes is a great leadership skill to have.

Hire Women and POCs: Companies with greater gender diversity were 1.4 times more likely to have demonstrated sustained, profitable growth". Put basically, companies lead by women make increasingly more money and isn't that what we all want? In addition to that, companies with an inclusive workplace culture have better employee retention.

Keep stress down: 76% of employees say that stress at work is negatively impacting their personal relationships. There are times when things may go wrong or get hectic around the workplace because of workload and deadlines. Handle these situations as proactively as possible. See a stressful time as an opportunity to present your leadership skills and use your resources to put together a problem-solving plan. Provide employees with material on how to reduce stress and prevent burn out. Our HR solutions can definitely alleviate that stress for you.

Know when to ask for help. How you approach challenges demonstrates your ability to address a difficult situation. Turn your challenges into opportunities. Being able to adapt to change is a necessity for company leaders to ensure longevity. Part of being a good leader is knowing when to ask for help.

Why don't employees take initiative?

Before you, as a leader or manager, pull your hair out because you feel as if you must 'spoon-feed' your people, answer these questions:

- Are they new graduates who are inexperienced and may not know what your expectations are and that you want them to show initiative?
- Are they scared of making mistakes for fear of getting into trouble and so tend to behave on the side of caution, and thus apathy?
- Is the culture in your team or Organisation one of power and control, where people are fearful to 'do the wrong' thing? If you have a culture where mistakes are not tolerated and people are berated for making mistakes, don't ask them to take initiative. They won't.
- Are you a leader who is unpredictable in your behaviour and your people are unsure how you will act on any day – thus are less likely to try new and different things?
- Some people are 'plodders' – they will never take initiative as it's not in their make-up. They are happy to be told what to do and how, but it places greater stress on leaders and managers.

Ways to encourage your Employees to take Initiative

1. **Create a safe, achievement-orientated culture** – your people need to know that you are a proactive and innovative Company that thrives on challenges. Mistakes are tolerated as long as they are learned from.

2. **Set exciting goals** – set goals that are high, but achievable. Make it fun and create an environment where scores are regularly tallied with a gong or bell, for example. This way, people see when goals are achieved, and a sense of collaboration is fostered.

3. **Hang with your people** – talk to them, show interest in them and get excited about the new 'way of being', sharing ideas with them.

4. **Create a culture of experimentation** – let people know that innovation is good and welcomed and that mistakes give you all a great platform from which to learn.

5. **Keep it simple** – don't overdo it. Just keep the rules simple and reward people for their contribution.

6. **Reward achievers** – tying in to creating goals and ways to publicly see when they are achieved (like a bell), create simple and achievable rewards for your people – movie tickets, money, days off etc.

7. **Lead by example** – get involved, get pumped and positive. Tell your people how much you value them showing initiative and doing things without being prompted

8. **Celebrate achievements** – cakes, certificates and giving awards are examples of showing people you appreciate their efforts, which keeps them motivated.

9. **Have fun** – there is no better place to work everyday than a fun and enjoyable working environment.

Be the proactive leader, who encourages your people to 'give things a go', encourage them to see opportunities, become boundary-less and reward them handsomely when they succeed. Not only with money. Praise often does just fine. Energetic, engaged and innovative employees are like gold. Make sure you keep them shining. Pure Magic International Business Solutions is an award-winning company, passionate about helping clients achieve strategic business outcomes through leadership, management and people development strategies and techniques at all levels by using a range of easy to implement HR and Organisational development strategies

Team initiative is positively related to team productivity: This is intended to be the first contribution of this work, to analyze how team initiative contributes to improving productivity. However, productivity should not be the only result to take into account; under the framework of positive psychology, it is also important to focus on the well-being of employees and not only on the absence of discomfort (in the form of burnout or stress or absenteeism, etc.), in this case, continuing at the work-team level with the concept of team work engagement.

Team Work Engagement: The concepts of work engagement and personal initiative have been studied in separate studies by authors who have minimal contact with one another. At least three different studies have shown positive relationships between work engagement and personal initiative. Work engagement is defined as a positive, fulfilling, work-related state of mind characterized by vigor, dedication, and absorption. Team work engagement is a shared, positive, and fulfilling, motivational emergent state of work that is related to well-being, defined similarly to individual level work engagement. Research that relates work engagement and personal initiative considers work engagement an antecedent or modulator/mediator variable.

Authentic leadership is positively related to team initiative: Numerous empirical studies have found that authentic leadership promotes multiple positive attitudes and behaviors that improve employee performance. Studies have shown that authentic leadership is positively related to organizational commitment, follower satisfaction with a supervisor, work performance, greater follower creativity and individual psychological capital, perceived team effectiveness, and followers' extra effort or higher levels of follower's performance. In addition, authentic leadership is negatively related to burnout and with higher work engagement. The role of the leader should be supporting teams to take action and to develop new ideas, encouraging team members to increase work engagement and achieve better productivity. However, the relationship between leadership and productivity has not received as much attention compared with other relationships. Recently, new leadership models have been proposed that could better relate to the current setting, which would allow a more precise understanding of leadership's influence on productivity.

Give teammates the opportunity to achieve without the fear of failure: The communication style of the leader will either encourage or discourage initiative by the people they supervise. Fear may work in the short-term to get people to do something, but over the long run, I believe personal pride is a much greater motivator. It produces far better results that last for a much longer time.

The leader encourages initiative when they hold people accountable and correct rather than criticize. Criticism and correction differ especially when it comes to methods and motives. Criticism puts someone down. Correction means I want to help. Be slow to correct and quick to commend. No one likes correction, but we learn from it. If we commend before we correct, the person will accept the correction better. But we must listen before we correct. There is usually another side to every story. If we listen to others, they will be more apt to listen to us.

It is very important how correction is given. We must be careful how we do it. We don't want those being corrected to lose face. Here are some good tips: Make it meaningful, but use judgment. Don't fly off the handle and be quick to correct. Do it with tact. If we just let fly, it is more likely to be viewed as criticism than as correction. Approval is a greater motivator than disapproval, but we have to disapprove on occasion when we correct. It's necessary. I only make corrections after I have proved to the individual that I highly value them. If they know we care for them, our correction won't be seen as judgment. I also tried to never make it personal. The leader who encourages initiative has faith in people. They believe in them, and thus draw out the best in them. If the initiative of the team member produces fruitful results, the leader gives away the credit. If it doesn't, the leader takes the blame.

Communicate clearly and Listen to Feedback: For teams to take initiative toward the fulfillment of goals, they need to know what those goals are. As a leader, you must tell your team members what the organizational goals are, and *why* those goals are what they are. At the same time, you must be willing to listen to feedback from your team. Team members may have questions about certain goals, and you should be able to answer them without becoming defensive. Moreover, it's worth your while to consider their feedback. As the people who are closest to the actual work, they often have good ideas about better ways to accomplish objectives. If you only talk and don't listen, you can miss out on some great ideas.

Setting Goals while Setting an Example: Part of your work as a leader involves setting goals. You know the organizational goals and the role your team is supposed to play. But merely setting the goals isn't enough. As a leader, you must set an example through your commitment to the goals and through your behavior as a leader. The best leaders design their lives and their work around their obligations to others, striving to become better people and demonstrating that they themselves will put in the work necessary to achieve goals. Developing teams that take initiative is really a matter of developing a better corporate culture. When the culture consistently shows the value of taking initiative, people and teams pick up on that and act accordingly. Conversely, when a company says it wants initiative, but then undermines it or actively discourages reasonable risk-taking, teams quickly pick up on that and initiative fizzles out. Leadership is the single most important factor in strong corporate culture, and it is a principle that I have worked with as part of many leadership coaching situations. Leaders may be competent and eager to lead effectively, yet they may not realize just how strong their influence is on their teams. Leadership coaching can assist leaders in understanding not only how to fulfill their potential, but how important it is to understand how they are perceived by those they lead. Today's businesses can't afford to forego initiative. Every day, companies develop innovations that threaten to disrupt entire industries, and companies without initiative-taking teams cannot compete effectively for very long. The quality of leadership is a key determinant of how eagerly teams embrace taking initiative.

CHAPTER FIFTEEN

Work Life Balance

Balancing your professional and personal life can be challenging, but it's essential. Often, work takes precedence over everything else in our lives. Our desire to succeed professionally can push us to set aside our own well-being. Creating a harmonious work-life balance or work-life integration is critical, though, to improve not only our physical, emotional and mental well-being, but it's also important for our career.

In short, work-life balance is the state of equilibrium where a person equally prioritizes the demands of one's career and the demands of one's personal life. Some of the common reasons that lead to a poor work-life balance include:

- Increased responsibilities at work
- Working longer hours
- Increased responsibilities at home
- Having children

A good work-life balance has numerous positive effects, including less stress, a lower risk of burnout and a greater sense of well-being. This not only benefits employees but employers, too. Employers who are committed to providing environments that support work-life balance for their employees can save on costs, experience fewer cases of absenteeism, and enjoy a more loyal and productive workforce. Employers that offer options as telecommuting or flexible work schedules can help employees have a better work-life balance. When creating a schedule that works for you, think about the best way to achieve balance at work and in your personal life. Work-life balance is less about dividing the hours in your day evenly between work and personal life and, instead, is more about having the flexibility to get things done in your professional life while still having time and energy to enjoy your personal life. There may be some days where you work longer hours so you have time later in the week to enjoy other activities.

I think the terms 'work-life balance' or 'work-life integration' are overused in the tech industry. I prefer to use the term 'work-life awareness'. The point is being mindful of how your work and your personal life overlap and integrate, and when they need to separate. It's difficult to build this awareness, especially in a fast-paced environment like the tech industry. Senior leaders are in demanding roles that can encompass their whole life. This makes it essential to create your own way of carrying yourself in your personal and professional life, which can cascade to your teams as well.

Why mostly leaders Struggles with Work-Life Balance: Work-life balance can be difficult for those in leadership positions to achieve. They have worked hard to reach positions of heightened visibility, influence, and accountability, and taking any time away from that could feel like a step backward, or like admitting vulnerability. There can be a large amount of responsibility placed on the shoulders of organizational leaders, since they are often not only responsible for taking care of their employees and the business, but also for managing owner or stockholder expectations. Addressing mental health for executives and professionals can be challenging because many assume that those who "have it all" are in complete control of every facet of their lives and their careers — this is not always the case. If you are constantly focused on your work, it can be hard to prioritize your life outside of work, and this can lead to CEO burnout and poor managerial decisions. All levels of employees struggle with similar issues, but when you are at the top, it can feel like focusing on yourself is unacceptable, or could subject you to scrutiny.

Benefits of Work-Life Balance: There are a number of compelling reasons for leaders to pursue a work-life balance, but the benefits are not mutually exclusive. Creating an organization with a culture that supports and enables work-life balance also confers benefits for its employees and the business as a whole — examples include:

- **Fight Burnout**: Emphasizing work-life balance helps combat employee burnout. When you mitigate employee burnout, you reduce the costs of employee turnover;
- **Improve Productivity**: There are physical and cognitive consequences of fatigue. By promoting work-life balance you are addressing issues of

fatigue. This can help you can boost performance and productivity;

- **Build a Better Brand**: Promoting positive work-life balance can create a positive workplace culture and improve brand perception. This can help with retaining employees as mentioned above, but it can also help with recruiting new employees, especially those from generations who greatly value work-life balance;
- **Foster Trust**: Trusting that your employees will accomplish tasks autonomously, regardless of how conventional their workday is, can help develop a culture of trust. This can enhance job satisfaction, transparency, and success within individual roles.

Taking time away from work helps people do better work: There's a simple solution to workplace stress... stop working for a bit. Humans need vacations. Even a little time away from work can help us relax and recharge. In fact, research shows that planned time away from work helps people do better work. In a Harvard study, 55% of people surveyed returned to work with much higher levels of energy after a low-stress vacation. Effective leaders inspire the people around them to push themselves to greatness. They lead by example, and you can set one for your team by maintaining a good work-life balance. Keeping the line between productivity and stress clear lets your employees know that they matter, and improves work quality all around.

Ways to create a better work-life balance, as well as how to be a supportive manager.

Accept that there is no 'perfect' work-life balance: When you hear work-life balance, you probably imagine having an extremely productive day at work, and leaving early to spend the other half of the day with friends and family. While this may seem ideal, it is not always possible. Don't strive for the perfect schedule; strive for a realistic one. Some days, you might focus more on work, while other days you might have more time and energy to pursue your hobbies or spend time with your loved ones. Balance is achieved over time, not each day. It is important to remain fluid and constantly assess where you are [versus] your goals and priorities," said Heather Monahan, founder of the career mentoring group. At times, your children may need you, and other times, you may need to travel for work, but allowing yourself to remain open to redirecting and assessing your needs on any day is key in finding balance.

Find a job that you love: Although work is an expected societal norm, your career shouldn't be restraining. If you hate what you do, you aren't going to be happy, plain and simple. You don't need to love every aspect of your job, but it needs to be exciting enough that you don't dread getting out of bed every morning. Finding a job that you are so passionate about you would do it for free. If your job is draining you, and you are finding it difficult to do the things you love outside of work, something is wrong. You may be working in a toxic environment, for a toxic person, or doing a job that you truly don't love. If this is the case, it is time to find a new job.

Prioritize your health: You're overall physical, emotional and mental health should be your main concern. If you struggle with anxiety or depression and think therapy would benefit you, fit those sessions into your schedule, even if you have to leave work early or ditch your evening spin class. If you are battling a chronic illness, don't be afraid to call in sick on rough days. Overworking yourself prevents you from getting better, possibly causing you to take more days off in the future. Prioritizing your health first and foremost will make you a better employee and person. You will miss less work, and when you are there, you will be happier and more productive. Prioritizing your health doesn't have to consist of radical or extreme activities. It can be as simple as daily meditation or exercise.

Don't be afraid to unplug: Cutting ties with the outside world from time to time allows us to recover from weekly stress and gives us space for other thoughts and ideas to emerge. Unplugging can mean something simple like practicing transit meditation on your daily commute, instead of checking work emails.

Take a vacation: Sometimes, truly unplugging means taking vacation time and shutting work completely off for a while. Whether your vacation consists of a one-day staycation or a two-week trip to your favorite destination, it's important to take time off to physically and mentally recharge. Employees are often worried that taking time off will disrupt the workflow, and they will be met with a backlog of work when they return. This fear should not restrict you from taking a much-needed break. The truth is, there is no nobility in not taking well-deserved time away from work; the benefits of taking a day off far outweigh the downsides. With proper planning, you can take time away without worrying about burdening your colleagues or contending with a huge workload when you return.

Make time for yourself and your loved ones: While your job is important, it shouldn't be your entire life. You were an individual before taking this position, and you should prioritize the activities or hobbies that make you happy. Achieving work-life balance requires deliberate action. If you do not firmly plan for personal time, you will never have time to do other things outside of work. No matter how hectic your schedule might be, you ultimately have control of your time and life.

When planning time with your loved ones, create a calendar for romantic and family dates. It may seem weird to plan one-on-one time with someone you live with, but it will ensure that you spend quality time with them without work-life conflict. Just because work keeps you busy doesn't mean you should neglect personal relationships. Realize that no one at your company is going to love you or appreciate you the way your loved ones do. "Also [remember] that everyone is replaceable at work, and no matter how important you think your job is, the company will not miss a beat tomorrow if you are gone."

Set boundaries and work hours: Set boundaries for yourself and your colleagues, to avoid burnout. When you leave the office, avoid thinking about upcoming projects or answering company emails. Consider having a separate computer or phone for work, so you can shut it off when you clock out. If that isn't possible, use separate browsers, emails or filters for your work and personal platforms. Additionally, setting specific work hours. Whether you work away from home or at home, it is important to determine when you will work and when you will stop working; otherwise, you might find yourself answering work-related emails late at night, during vacations or on weekends off. Notifying team members and your manager about boundaries beyond which you cannot be accessible because you are engaged in personal activities. This will help to ensure that they understand and respect your workplace limits and expectations.

Set goals and priorities (and stick to them): Set achievable goals by implementing time-management strategies, analyzing your to-do list, and cutting out tasks that have little to no value. Pay attention to when you are most productive at work and block that time off for your most important work-related activities. Avoid checking your emails and phone every few minutes, as those are major time-wasting tasks that derail your attention and productivity. Structuring your day can increase productivity at work, which can result in more free time to relax outside of work.

Be a supportive manager: To help managers do a better job of supporting their employees' efforts to achieve a healthier work-life balance

1. **Know what your employees are striving for.** Not everyone has the same work-life balance goals. Talk to each employee about their objectives, and then determine what you can do to help them. Some employees may benefit from working remotely a couple of days each week, while others may prefer altering their daily work schedule. It's important to be open-minded and flexible.

1. **Set a good example.** Your employees follow your lead. If you send emails at all hours of the day and night or work hard on the weekends, your staff thinks that is what is expected of them, too.

3. **Let employees know what their options are.** While employers typically do a good job of highlighting their work-life balance offerings to prospective job candidates, the same can't be said for communicating those initiatives to current employees. Regularly discuss with your employees the options that are available to them. Also, sit down with soon-to-be parents and discuss parental leave options.

4. **Stay at the forefront.** It is important to keep ahead of the curve on emerging work-life balance trends. What works today for employees might not be a good fit a year from now. Keep your work-life balance initiatives fresh, and offer in-demand benefits. Plus, consider offering work-life programs.

www.ingramcontent.com/pod-product-compliance
Lightning Source LLC
Chambersburg PA
CBHW070912160726
48004CB00003B/1334